Portrayed *Crazy*

a memoir of spousal abuse

Kate Klaver

River Lights Publishing
1098 Main St.
Dubuque, IA 52001

Book design by Alina Crow Designs
Cover design by Alina Crow Designs

Manufactured in the United States of America

ISBN: 978-0-9976849-7-1

Printed in the United States of America

To Jessica
Without your encouragement, my story may never
have come to light. Meeting you was meant to be.
Thank you for your empathy and compassion.

A big thank you to Andrea and River Lights Publishing
for giving me the platform to have my voice heard.

Contents

WHEN MY SECRETS FINALLY BROKE, many encouraged me to write a book. I hadn't thought my life had nosedived to that extent. Looking back, I hadn't realized just how out of control my marriage had gotten.

In efforts to help others understand and comprehend domestic violence, I'm sharing my story with sole intent to put perspective on spousal abuse.

Once shattered and broken from an abusive marriage, I have pieced myself whole again. Becoming tougher, candid, and often outspoken, inspired me to become an advocate against domestic violence. It is my intent that being proactive will prevent unnecessary future suffering to others.

At the time, my case was considered one of the worst cases of domestic violence recorded in Clark County, Iowa. Although there may have been worse cases in this county, they were not reported or documented for record.

Once a victim and now grateful survivor, 7 years have passed. Blessed to have regained emotional equilibrium and inner peace, I feel an obligation to speak up and out against spousal abuse.

For security purposes and legal reasons, efforts have been made to disguise names, addresses and towns to protect the innocent as well as the guilty. The individuals depicted may have different recollections than those I recalled.

My memoir doesn't depict my entire life story—only fragments, segments and situations I am telling truthfully and honestly per my memories. It is a compelling viewpoint on the taboo subject of spousal abuse, exposing all of myself and the dominance that controlled my entirety.

It is my intent as I bring my story to light that my voice resonates more awareness to other families whose loved ones are unable to help themselves escape abuse. Emotional, mental and psychological abuse often leads to physical violence. Abuser's threats of possessive retaliation keep victims in their place, isolated from family and friends. That deadly fear grips a victim from coming forward, exposing secrets.

This story of endurance, disclosure and resolution, is a telling account of vivid recollections purged during extensive counseling and therapy sessions. Having healed healthy, stronger and wiser, *Portrayed Crazy* exposes my difficult journey to freedom.

1

Courthouse

IT WAS HOURS BEFORE THE Clark County Courthouse would open that August morning in 2011, as I sat in my locked vehicle, mopping perspiration from the Iowa humidity that rivaled Florida's that summer. My eyes scanned the urban landscape of the tiny town, but I saw no sign of my husband, D. I was certain he was on his way though, and I was determined to beat him to the clerk. My hands shook, and I craved a cigarette, but had to settle for Nicorette® and chewed a new piece every 15 minutes. I did as my friend Jenna suggested and got out pen and paper to write down everything D had done to me.

I had to psych myself up for the purge. It was painful to admit the stupid reality of my life, born of a careless decision 36 years ago and reinforced by centuries of Catholic marital conviction to persevere at all costs. They were beliefs held fast by generations of my family who were country folk. My coarse hands shook as I wrote and I had to keep wiping my face so tears wouldn't drip on the notepad. With a long list and a memory that went back almost 40 years, where the hell would I begin? Too many secrets fired in my brain. He had vandalized my soul. How do you put that into words?

The what-ifs kept exploding in my head, making organized thought impossible. What if I don't get a judge to validate my claims? Then what kind of life would be waiting for me? I sure as hell couldn't go home because D would make sure I'd never see daylight again. My mind went to the attic room where there were no windows after he boarded them up with siding a few years earlier. The doorknob to the room was so old that from the inside it only spun. Once, early in our marriage, we used the room for storage and while looking for something, I got shut in. D had to let me out. I'll never forget his cackling laugh while he teased me before opening the door. Another time he flipped the lights off in the attic room. I have claustrophobia and I fear total darkness. D knew it. Again, he laughed.

Would anyone come looking for me in time? Doubtful.

And what if I don't get a protection order and D locks me out of the house? Would the police come? They were chummy with him.

On the notepad I scribbled a list of D's insults, belittlings, degradings, the walking me up against walls, the feeling of the refrigerator door handle against my back, the scraping of layers from my soul, and of how I had grown smaller as his ego had grown larger. D was dominating/controlling with every childish temper tantrum he threw.

What if I was actually fortunate enough to get a restraining order? Could I get that lucky? That would mean that D would be removed from our house. I had prayed for decades to escape from his temper. Now that this possibility loomed, I was having second thoughts because after the order expired, he would really be gunning for me. Then what?

By 7:30 a.m. my anxiety and the heat got the best of me and I had to get out of the car. I went and sat on the courthouse steps to wait out the last hour. The town was coming awake. Old, hunched farmers headed to the city café and trucks with loud mufflers drove by on their way to work.

No one seemed to notice me, though I felt as obvious as a fallen stalk of corn in a perfect row. The front door rattled, startling me as I turned to see an elderly janitor with a mop. I jumped to my feet and grabbed my purse, which was particularly heavy that day serving as a briefcase, duffel bag, and snack bar.

"Are you O.K.?" he asked.

"I'm here to file a protection order," I said, but it was more like the words exploded from my mouth.

"I'll let you in early, but the courthouse doesn't really open for another twenty minutes."

The janitor escorted me up to the second floor and pointed toward a wooden bench where I could wait until the Clerk of Court office opened. He went about his business, mopping the floors, swinging past me several times. After a brutal wait, the roll-top shutter rattled open at the clerk's window. I dashed to the counter.

"I'm here to file a protection order," I said, stepping on the clerk's salutation.

"I'm sorry ma'am we don't have a judge on Mondays," she said.

I held my breath as the blood drained from my face.

"Does that mean I can't get a protection order today?" I asked.

"That's correct," she said. "The judge has to sign the Order of Protection."

"Chief Preston from Sunton advised me that if I felt my life was in danger from my husband, I should file a protection order against him," I blurted. "And if I don't get one today, I'm going to be a dead woman." My demeanor was dissolving by the second.

The clerk touched my wrist and said, "It's going to be okay. We're here to help you."

"I know he's coming. He could be here any minute," I said.

An assistant to the clerk stepped forward and offered to escort me to another room where she advised me to remain quiet and to start filling in the blanks on the form for the Order of Protection.

Within minutes, two officers appeared in the doorway. One of them sat across the table from me and the other one guarded the door. I felt safer but knew they couldn't come home with me.

Hard as it was to write with my shaking hand, I managed to scribble the notes on the form. It seemed funny that that little piece of paper could possibly protect me and I didn't know if I could trust it. I froze when I heard D's voice on the other side of the wall.

Just then, the assistant tapped lightly on the door and entered my room.

"Shhh, he's out there," she whispered, holding her index finger to her lips.

I heard the muffled sound of D's voice say, "I'm here to get a protection order against my wife."

His words sucked the breath from me and my stomach pumped acid. But my resolve strengthened. Whatever happened next, I would either win or escape.

Blind Date

IN THE SUMMER OF 1975, I was two years out of high school. Life was uncomplicated and like most kids, I lived in the moment. It was the psychedelic age. The drink of the day was sangria or screwdrivers. We wore bell bottoms and fringed vests, got high on dope and speed, and jammed to Ozark Mountain Daredevils. It was an era and a place when you got a job instead of a college education and you would keep that job until you retired with a pension.

At the time, I had a best friend named Joannie, who was also my roommate. We confided in each other about everything and became close. It would be a friendship that would last to this day. Since I didn't have a car, I relied on Joannie for all rides from running errands to attending parties and events. Neither one of us had boyfriends and didn't care. I thought it would have been nice to be paired with someone, but I wasn't needy or desperate enough to barhop. I was content to be on my own.

One day, an unexpected phone call from a remote cousin would change the course of my life. She asked if I would like to go on a blind date with the brother of her boyfriend. I was apprehensive because I had never been on a blind date before, but in rural Iowa in the '70s, dirt roads and cornfields stretched forever, and excitement was hard to come by, so I accepted the offer.

I decided to make a memorable impression, with my summer tan on full display, by way of a halter top. My long brown hair, highlighted by the summer sun, cascaded down my back to my hip hugger jeans. I was nervous and excited at the same time, wondering about my date's appearance.

D, a 26-year-old man, pulled into my cousin's driveway that evening, loudly revving his muscle car to impress. I was immediately turned off by his juvenile behavior. He seemed to have no idea that his attire made him look like a hillbilly dressed for church. It was clear that the iron crease in the front of his jeans was important and one couldn't help but follow the crease down to his snazzy suede ankle boots, which were on full display because his jeans were hemmed too short. He had stringy blonde hair that stuck out from beneath his faded farmer's cap and a white t-shirt plastered with the Budweiser® logo. He was also rude. I had reached out my hand to introduce myself, but he didn't respond. It was then I noticed how large D's hands were—they were out of proportion to his small frame. I was disappointed in his appearance and crudeness, but I was a polite young woman and continued to act happy to meet him.

"You ready to go?" he asked, pivoting toward his car. I followed but split off when D continued to his side of the car. My cousin and D's brother decided to leave us to ourselves and they headed to their car. I helped myself to the front seat, wondering if he had ever learned to open a car door for a lady.

As we took off, D attempted to impress the entire neighborhood with the sound of his car. He appeared to be unaware that I was in the car. I felt ignored and undesirable. He switched radio stations without regard for my taste in music as we roared past the green cornfields in the 20-mile stretch to D's favorite tavern. We chain-smoked cigarettes along the way to look cool and we sweated in the August heat since the car had no air conditioning.

The Sunton Bar was filled to capacity with construction workers, farmers, and other locals. The jukebox blared as D strode in ahead of me like a cock with his banty.

Relaxed in his element, D began to work the crowd with stories that sounded like exaggerations, but which were bought fully by the friends that had gathered. I stood behind him, feeling awkward because I didn't know anyone. He acted like I wasn't there. At one point, he left me standing alone to figure out where I could hide myself. Others glanced and stared, but no one bothered to make me feel welcome.

From my vantage point I could see D digging in his back pocket for his billfold. He ordered himself a cold one and glanced over his shoulder, hollering over the loud volume of the crowd.

"What do you want to drink?"

"I'll have a screwdriver," I yelled, answering back, impressed he would offer.

After delivering my drink, D pulled up the only available stool to lounge at the bar and I looked around the smoked-filled establishment for a place to sit. An empty corner booth would work until D joined me. He walked past me several times to use the restroom, but with the place being so crowded, he either didn't see me or he was testing to see if I would come to him first. I should've moseyed up to the bar and introduced myself to get acquainted with others, but I was on D's stomping ground, and decided to remain low-key instead. As I people-watched, I tried to get a feel for his world of bar drinking that included loud music, vulgarity, and fights over the pool table. I couldn't understand the appeal, but felt that those who were drinking heavily had the better understanding. Sure enough, I appeared to be the only sober one there.

Congregating to get drunk and brag of vomiting and hangovers the next day was standard procedure for our age. Thirsty young men met at their favorite watering holes while their women trailed behind, meeting up with other girlfriends to watch their boyfriends make fools of themselves. I couldn't relate to the idea that a few hours of fun were worth a horrible hangover with no recollection of the night before. Family problems with alcoholism had taught me to rarely touch alcohol. Out of my element, I slouched further into the booth waiting for D to remember I was there.

Hours passed, and the tavern began to empty with the exception of a few diehards and D, who had staked claim to the end of the bar. The entire evening I sat in the corner booth, nursing a watered-down screwdriver, witnessing firsthand D's usual weekend entertainment. The drunker D got, the more disgusting I found him. Although I despised his childish behavior and the way he neglected me, it wasn't worth the argument to let him know how I felt because I was sure I would never see him again. In a burst of drunken revelation, D's face turned sideways, staring directly at me. It was at that moment his brain seemed to form the conclusion that he had forgotten all about me as I sat alone, fed up with him.

He came weaving toward me, his feet stepping high.

"Oh, there you are. Been looking for you," he said, trying to hold his head straight. It was obvious that he only noticed me now that no one else was around.

Irked by his smugness, I could feel my face turn red. D flopped into the seat across from me and stared at my empty glass.

"How many of those did you suck down tonight?" he asked, trying to make conversation as his head bobbed like a buoy.

"This is the same one you bought me hours ago," I said.

I could tell what I said didn't register with him.

There was a good minute or so of silence and then D said, "Whew. I had a really fuckin' good time tonight. You ready to go?"

"Yeah. I . . ." but D cut in.

"I've got to get going 'cause I got a lot of shit to do tomorrow around the house."

"Don't you have a bunch of brothers who can help?" I asked.

"Are you fuckin' kidding me? They're worthless."

I was shocked by D's demeaning of his family but said nothing.

He tried to fill the air between us, and told melancholy stories about his family problems. Most of his stories depicted how poor his family had been and that he, and only he, out of his entire family, was supporting his mother financially. It surely was a heavy burden to carry all alone, I thought.

"What does your dad do for a living?" I asked.

D tearfully slurred, "I don't have a fuckin' old man."

I assumed that his father had passed, and I felt sorry for him as I remained silent.

His stories of poverty, particularly, gripped my heart. According to D, his family was on welfare and he had had to work since the age of 16. My picture of him began to change as I imagined the struggle of his large family without a father and an arthritic, disabled mother at the helm. In his inebriated state, he flipped from his slumped demeanor into a puffed-chested braggart, as "father" of the family.

"Yup, I'm man of the house," he slurred. "If it wasn't for me, my six brothers and five sisters would be in a fuckin' orphanage."

His words pulled at my heart. I didn't know who to feel more sorry for, him or his poor mother with all those children to raise.

D continued pitying himself. "None of them got a pot to piss in."

"Oh. That must be hard on you," I replied.

"Damn right. I'm the boss of the house," he boasted. "When I bark orders, by God, my sisters and brothers jump."

I tried to imagine shouldering such a heavy load, although it dawned on me that it could have been the liquor talking. Nevertheless, I found myself feeling sorry for him that he had to take on so much responsibility at such a young age.

"How long have you been the dad of the family?"

"Since I was sixteen."

"Sixteen?" I said. "Oh my God."

"Yup. I had to quit school to help out."

I was aghast. Although D was pitifully drunk, I admired him for his drive to keep the family together. I overlooked his sarcasm and chalked his rudeness up to the liquor.

During that first date I went from being repulsed by him to being captivated by him for his hard-luck story. I believed in my heart I could soften his coarseness and perhaps I could connect to a tender soul, beneath that façade, if I accepted a second date.

Not to mention, he had a car.

Born and Bred

A CAR WAS A TICKET to excitement in the Corn Belt where life was fraught with boredom. D had that going for him and being with someone was better than being with no one. It wasn't like I had a choice in men. It was a day and age when you settled for a convenient partner. A perfectly good girl could throw her youth away by never meeting an available man. We were also Catholic and the code to stay committed was all but branded on our butt cheeks.

Living in the country and growing up on the farm was all my family ever knew. My parents were from big Catholic families and they did what their parents did, they grew large families, a tradition that suited Catholicism and farm life both. I was the third child, and my parents continued growing their brood until it reached twelve.

My father worked the land of our century-old farm that had been passed on by his father. My mother was raised in a small town and enjoyed finer things before moving to the farm with my father. I can only imagine how rough it must have been for her to adjust to country living, home 24/7, stuck with so many mouths to feed and mountains of laundry to do. Back then, a farm wife rarely had a social life. She was too busy tending kids, washing, and canning. My mother was a modest, non-confrontational woman to a fault. She bowed to my father and was forever willing to sweep all his bad behavior from being a mean drunk, under the rug.

When I was in my middle teens, before my father began to drink, he was a decent man. He was a bright guy who could fix any broken mechanical device. He started his own electrical business on the side, wiring homes, buildings, and grain bins. We knew if something broke we could always go to Dad to get it fixed. While he was generous and kind in that way, he was strict, as all parents were, and he made it clear that there were consequences for bad behavior. It could be either a denial of a privilege punishment, or a whipping. We were obedient because we feared him. He was fair and impartial in his punishments, with none of us getting more than another.

As I got into my late teens, my father began to drink often and plenty. His methods of keeping us in line became more severe and his overreactions to annoyances became easier to trigger. The frequency of punishments with a belt, in vulgarity-laced tirades began to increase. First, he would insist the offender lay over the kitchen chair and then he would whip his belt from its loops. After doubling the belt, he'd deliver at least three good whacks to our butt cheeks or legs. Though we weren't required to remove our pants, it would leave welts.

No matter how unjust the sentence, you were never to defend yourself. One time, when I was 25 years old and living on my own, I stopped by my parents' house for a visit and was telling my father that I wanted a dog. Out of the blue, he beckoned me toward him where he was sitting drunk at the kitchen counter. He kept insisting I get closer and when I got near his face, he grabbed both sides of my long hair and violently yanked my head into the counter, smashing my nose, chin, and forehead.

"You don't need a goddamn dog," he shouted. I was so shocked, pained, and humiliated that I hated him in the moment. But I said nothing, and took the punishment like my mother took it from her father, and like her mother took it before her.

Though it seems extreme looking back, and would be considered child abuse or assault today, at the time, incidents like this would blow over and we would be back to life as normal by the next day. That's the way families worked, and no one questioned it.

Church was every Sunday from birth. We all dressed in our church clothes with strict attention to detail. Hair had to be combed just right or you were sent back into the house. We went through the motions of memorizing the mass in

Latin, understanding nothing, knowing only that God was our savior and whatever the Pope and Priest said, reigned supreme. We were taught never to question authority.

But like many farm kids, I couldn't wait to move away after graduation in 1973. From the dusty roads, the enormous cooking and baking schedule, cleaning, laundry and mowing the lawn maze that covered the farm, I had seen how my mother struggled with everything and I wanted a better life for myself.

I accepted a second date. From that point on, seeing D on Friday and Saturday became a regular thing. He would drive to Manley to pick me up, and we would drive back to Sunton to hit the bar. He would then drive me home in his inebriated state. In those days, we didn't worry about getting caught driving under the influence and believed we were invincible and lucky.

Watching D get drunk enough to start a fight was still better than sitting in my apartment watching *Six Million Dollar Man* or *Police Woman*. The drunker he got, the bigger the chip on his shoulder and the easier it was to dislodge it.

In 1975, bar-brawling in Iowa for restless youths was not unusual and was often part of the evening's entertainment for muscled construction workers and tough farm boys. D would often instigate a fight and rely on his brothers for back up. While his affinity for settling a score with violence should have been a warning sign to me, I didn't think much of it then, having grown up with nine brawling brothers. It was the way they established hierarchy in the boondocks where words were for sissies and the size of your truck mattered more than the size of your education. When I would ask D what the arguments were about, he dismissed them as nothing more than work related. Yet, the next day he would boast of his fighting accomplishments, sending the message to others not to mess with him.

Over the course of three months, I continued to date D and waste long nights at the Sunton bar. Even though we became known as 'a couple,' I couldn't dismiss everything about him that bothered me. I got nothing from D in the way of affection or kindness. A single compliment would have gone a long way, but he was stingy. I couldn't justify going on and knew it was time to end it.

I wasn't looking forward to breaking the news to D. We had our usual date planned to go to the Sunton Bar one Friday night when D came to pick me up. I invited him in and we sat on the sofa to chat. I told him I had something to say. It was obvious he never saw it coming and his reaction was extreme.

He glared at me and he leapt from the sofa causing me to leap as well.

"Oh. I ain't good enough for you now?" he hollered, walking me up against the living room wall.

Taken off-guard by his quick temper, I stuttered, "Ah no. No. That's not what I said."

The rage from his bruised ego exploded. I attempted to calm the situation, toning my voice to a whisper but he refused to hear.

Index finger pointed inches from my nose, he spewed words, twisting them to fit his anger.

"The fuck you didn't. I know damn well what I heard."

I could smell the alcohol and wondered how many drinks he downed before he had gotten to my place. It was impossible to reason with D sober much less when alcohol fueled his senses.

"No D, that's not what I said. I said maybe dating other people wouldn't be such a bad idea."

I tried inching sideways from him, but he got back in my face.

"The hell you didn't you lying bitch," he cussed, getting in the last word as he jerked away.

Tromping through the kitchen, he grabbed the front door handle, flinging my apartment door wide open and tossing another "BITCH" over his shoulder on his way out.

It was the first time I witnessed his quick fuse. His tantrum continued to unfurl as he stomped down the narrow steps from my apartment. I was stunned and had seen D mad enough to fight but had assumed he would not turn rage on me. His short fuse began to scare me.

As he reached the bottom, he took out his hostility on the door and punched the screen. It made me nervous enough to whisk myself into my apartment, quickly locking the door behind me.

I ran to the front picture window just in time to see D scurrying to reach his car door, kicking dirt, and mumbling obscenities as he went. God and Jesus were part of his rant. Revving his car engine for the town to hear, he shifted into reverse, lurching backward, kicking up rocks in the gravel driveway. He punched his engine into overdrive. When he got to the asphalt, the street wore down his tires with a high-pitched squeal, leaving the black evidence behind as stripes on the road.

I got a grip on myself, relieved D was gone. After all the crap, I was glad our relationship was over. We weren't compatible. I might not have had big goals in life, but I surely couldn't see myself with this crass man who never seemed to grow up or own his mistakes.

I would learn that no one said "no" to D. I didn't know it at the time, but he wasn't about to let me go. He brooded for several weeks without any contact. Because I didn't hear from him, I assumed D found another girl to use. Self-doubt began to grow, and I wondered if I had overreacted. Did I cause his temper tantrum? I didn't think so, as I had tried to let D down gently, but guilt gnawed at me.

One night, a soft knock on my front door revealed a sheepish looking D. With a trucker's cap intentionally pulled over his eyes, he stared at the floor with his hands shoved in his jean pockets. A toothpick wedged between his front teeth bounced up and down. My eyes surveyed his body language to discover his intent. He was quiet and subdued and appeared too reserved for his scruffy mentality. I found myself feeling bad that I had provoked him to bitterly peel away from my driveway weeks earlier.

D cleared his throat and grunted a greeting. He edged forward as I stepped back, unsure what he would do. Perspiration wet my upper lip, but his demeanor now seemed low-key and he didn't appear to be in a fighting mood. My face was blank as I waited for a clue.

With his eyes buried under his cap bill, out of nowhere a mysterious small cardboard box appeared in D's hands.

"Here," he said, handing me the unexpected gift. With poor communication skills, D seemed to believe that buying me something would negate his bad behavior.

"Well ahh we've been together three months now and this is for being my girlfriend."

I was stunned as I tried to process what he said, and hesitated to open the box, wondering how I had gotten myself into such an awkward position.

His two-way personality turned impatient before my fingers could open the box lid.

"Come on. Open the damn thing," he blurted, impatient to seize the moment.

Smelling alcohol on his breath, I questioned how many D had downed to find the courage to come knocking at my door with a gift. I wondered if he had ever gone one day of his adult life without booze. For D though, he had to liquor himself up to inflate his ego. I was naïve to believe that I was good for him, and that I might be able to get him to cut back on his drinking.

I could only stare at the box cupped between my fingers.

"Well go ahead and see what I bought you for going steady with me," he said with growing agitation. Back then, 'going steady' meant practically married. "I'll find somebody else who appreciates it since I ain't good enough for you."

I would have preferred an apology in the form of two little words, but those words were not part of his crude vocabulary. Nervous about his heated temper and wondering if he'd huff and puff from my apartment again if he didn't get his way, I relented and unhinged the box. Inside was a topaz ring. I had never mentioned my November birthday to him, so I was quite surprised that it was the color of my birthstone. I wondered if he had just gotten lucky.

I didn't want to accept his buy-off apology. However, seeing that amber-colored stone sucked me back into his sphere. My life sat on a pivot as he told me to put on the ring. Little did I know, as I forced it over the knuckle of my right ring finger, that I was sealing my fate for the next 36 years. Blinded by his momentary generosity and his good faith attempt to prove himself worthy, however crude, I let myself slip into an imaginary bond of compassion.

Before I knew it, D told me his mother wanted to meet me and invited me for Sunday dinner. It was the first time I had ever been invited home by a guy and it felt like a real relationship. I was excited to meet his mother and the rest of his family.

D picked me up that day and when we arrived at his house, I was surprised by the size of the large Victorian mansion that sat on a large weed-filled lot. As we entered the back porch, the smell of pot roast wafted from the kitchen and we were greeted by a number of D's youngest siblings, all hyped with excitement over their new guest. Though D and I had the same number of siblings, I was surprised by how noisy and chaotic their home was compared to my family's. His siblings showed off, argued, and fought freely. Without a father, and with a passive mother, there seemed to be no control other than D ordering them about as the authority figure. Nevertheless, his mother and the kids were all kind to me. The long dining room table was set with white linen and the meal that ensued was bountiful. There was joy in the air and it felt good as we bowed our heads to D's prayer before eating. I was smitten by his fun-loving family that seemed smitten by me in return.

As if the meal to meet his family had staked his claim to me, D began to pressure me to have sex. It took a lot of coaxing from him, but eventually I gave in. We consummated our relationship. This furthered our bond.

It wasn't long before D used me as his designated driver, to haul his drunken ass around. I would take him back to my house where he would pass out and sometimes he would be so out of it he would lose control of his bladder and bowels. The odor made me gag and I would sleep facing the other direction as far to the edge of the bed as possible. I never brought it up to D so as not to embarrass or infuriate him and I would dutifully wash the bedclothes as I swept the problem under the rug. After a while the mattress became stained and stank too. Decades later during our divorce, when disposing of that same mattress, he would publicly embarrass me by telling others I was the one who soiled it.

The Follower

PER MY OLD-SCHOOL UPBRINGING, I felt comfortable with letting D make all of our decisions. It was a tradition steeped in me from generations past. I didn't question it because it felt normal.

Once I was all in with D, I began to mimic his ways. If he hated someone, I hated them. If he referred to the "fuckin' something," I referred to the "fuckin' something." I ate what he ate and I did what he wanted. It was easier to give in than to argue back. I had learned to fear D's anger when he didn't get his way. I didn't realize at the time how lopsided the relationship was getting. I was losing my sense of self as I became fixated on pleasing D, pumping his ego with compliments, and maintaining the status quo.

D had given me strict instructions as to what I could and couldn't say to other people and I wasn't allowed to discuss any family problems that pertained to him. I obeyed to avoid invoking D's ire. As time went on, to be safe, I spoke less and less at social gatherings, afraid I would say the wrong thing. I began to notice that D's relatives distanced themselves from me as if I was being unfriendly.

There was also an uptick in my being the brunt of D's jokes. He thought nothing of pointing out my flaws to others, calling me "lard-ass" and other insulting names.

For the 11 years that I dated D before we got married, softball ruled our lives because D liked to play. It trumped everything I wanted to do because I was always required to be with him and often had to forfeit other plans. After 10 of those 11 years, the team finally dissolved due to burnout. I was relieved.

Almost a decade into dating D, I had grown tired of our arrangement and one day, I decided to ask him about our future. I told him I wanted to be married like the rest of our families and friends and that we continued going nowhere in our relationship. He'd promised to marry me but claimed the time was wrong because he couldn't support two women at once: his mother and me. He assured me that after the last sibling graduated from high school, we'd get married. Fed up with those years coming and going, I finally confronted him with his broken promise. To my surprise, shortly thereafter, we went looking for a wedding ring. We didn't get an engagement ring, only a band for me. D refused one for himself, claiming a band would be hazardous to his hand in his profession. I didn't see how, and let it go. Since he was paying for the ring, he made the final decision on which one. I felt no emotion during the process of picking out a wedding ring. It should have been another warning sign.

I also felt no emotion when I stuffed the box in my bedroom dresser drawer for the next few months, pending our engagement announcement scheduled for Christmas Eve. I wanted to be married but I had trouble buying into the idea that D was a good match. Still, I pushed forward, doing what others expected me to do because that was all I knew, and I had 10 years invested in D.

Neither side of our families appeared happy for me when I broke the news that we were getting married. D required me to plan my own wedding as cheap as possible as he began to control every aspect of our big day. He ordered me to eliminate my sisters, Evie and Ava, from our wedding party, arguing that they weren't close enough to me to be in the wedding party. I balked because I was a bridesmaid in both their weddings years earlier and wanted to return the honor. I was concerned that this would drive a bigger wedge between us since relations were already tenuous. I had even considered that making my sisters bridesmaids would bring us closer. An argument ensued, and I gave the ring back.

For the first time, I stood my ground, giving him the silent treatment for two weeks. That would be the first of several times throughout our relationship and marriage that I would unsuccessfully attempt to break up with D. After a few weeks he called, told me he loved me and he promised to never let our families interfere in our lives. He had never told me that he loved me before. I was so shocked to hear such a rare display of emotion that my heart flipped again. I believed that there really was a kind side to him. Because D had given in, I gave in too, and agreed to choose other bridesmaids besides my sisters.

After months of planning our September wedding, D and I married in 1986. We feigned happiness and cozied up enough to disguise our dullness for one another on our big day. After 11 years of an empty relationship, the only emotion I felt on my wedding day was detachment. I felt like a bystander watching the spectacle unfold.

Though I had an uneasy feeling, I was too naïve to see that D would rob me of my best years. The whole time we were dating, D had lived with his mother. And now, I would be replacing her—cooking, cleaning and other subservient duties, becoming his robot, existing to serve D's every need. Over time, insomnia set in and I became more depressed as the empty relationship continued, and his over-bearing ways increased.

As our bond to each other became fixed, D reigned me in tighter with every dollar I spent. This included costs for long distance phone calls, mileage, and groceries. It was always something petty. He had become fanatical with 'his' money and scrutinized everything I did.

Even though my leash was tight, he became paranoid that I was doing something behind his back. He began to eavesdrop on my conversations with neighbors and interrogate me about phone calls I had had, reprimanding me for not saying just the right thing. I had nothing to hide and never lied to him, yet he found it necessary to tighten his control of me.

D had decided we would live in the same house his family grew up in, in the town of Sunton, after his aging mother could no longer manage the house by herself. It was a lovely old Victorian and I was on board with the decision.

Things continued to deteriorate between us and the outlook became bleak. Though I wasn't working outside the home, it was vital I busy myself to occupy my time. I did a thorough cleaning and painting of the old house starting with the third-floor, walk-in attic. Upon entering the attic, I found windows broken. With no broken glass inside, it was clear they had been busted from the inside out. This explained the flying bats in our living room at night. I suspected it was the result of resentment on the part of one of D's sisters who had lived in the house with their mother and was angry that she had to move out because D and I were going to take over the house. She was forever horrible to me after that and would call me bitch in front of others. D never tried to stop her.

Nothing in the house spoke of my personal touch. D was written all over everything. He wanted the house to remain the exact same as when his family had resided there. Change of any kind threw D off balance and put him in a tailspin of anger. Learning that, I slowly inserted my personal touch with money I received from unemployment benefits, making subtle changes here and there. I was always mindful to make sure the house was not in disarray when D returned home.

One day, a girlfriend helped wallpaper the walls in the bathroom. I had lost track of the time and when D arrived home from work that day, we were still in the midst of adding the last of the wallpaper strips and were giggling about something with music blaring.

Stomping into the kitchen giving me the evil eye, he leaned in my ear so my friend couldn't hear his nasty remark.

"Get this fuckin' shit cleaned up and now."

Staring down at his six pack of beer, with three cans missing, I could see he already drank his supper. I jumped to it in a cleaning frenzy and after my friend left, D tore into me with vulgar words, backing me to the wall with pointed fingers. He made it clear that he expected 'his' house immaculate at all times.

From then on, I eagled-eyed the clock each afternoon, obeying his rules in his house, his way.

In those early days of marriage, I taught myself to become thrifty. Detouring to any and all garage sales along the way to grocery shopping satisfied my need to want nice things at a fraction of the cost. Visiting Goodwill stores and retail outlets, I hunted bargains to fill voids in my marriage. While others bragged about brand name clothes, I had no shame calling myself master of frugality, scrounging free boxes of stuff and even dumpster diving. Dealt a frugal budget by my husband, I made the best of it, and even loved the challenge of finding great deals. I was determined to enjoy life just to spite him and in return, he was determined not to let me.

Tubal Ligation

ONE NIGHT, A FEW MONTHS into our marriage, after D's gratification was met and we both had turned away from each other to sprawl more comfortably for the night, I brought up the subject of kids. It was the first time we had ever broached the subject in more than eleven years together.

His response was swift and complete. "We ain't having no kids," he said.

"Well not now, but someday," I answered back.

His sweaty torso bolted into an upright position.

"I said, we ain't having kids. We talked about that. Don't you remember?"

My body tensed as I sat up to address him. I could tell he was storming for a fight.

"No. I don't remember. We never talked about kids," I replied as my spirits barreled south.

"Oh, yeah we did. Don't you remember? It was at pre-Cana classes, before we got married," said D. I was sure we had never discussed a subject that a woman would sear into her memory, but I could tell D was going to stick to his story and I already knew what that meant. By Catholic standards in those days, a priest refused to marry a couple unless they attended an all-day pre-Cana class consisting of an elderly husband and wife sharing their life's lessons of marriage. Without pre-Cana, the old-school church didn't recognize marriage.

I had assumed D wanted kids too. It was a big part of being Catholic and we were both from huge Catholic families. I couldn't even imagine D saying he didn't want children in pre-Cana class, for its anti-Catholic sentiment. The blood was draining from my face as reality dawned that I would never have children.

"But kids are part of having a family and we have the room with this big house."

"Where do you come up with this shit?" he shot back. "I ain't having any rug rats running around this house or we're getting a damn divorce. I told you that how many damn times," he scolded. "Your memory sucks." Whenever D told a lie, his response was to roll anger out as a means to override the lie.

For the very first time in our relationship, I pushed back, defending myself. My recollection and his recollection were complete opposites.

"No I didn't forget. I'd remember something as important as kids, D."

"No fuckin' kids or this ain't going to work. In fact, I made that perfectly clear right from the beginning when we first started dating. Don't you remember, I hated using rubbers," he said, making things up as he went. "So I told you to get on the damn pill when we first started having sex so you wouldn't get pregnant. I didn't want fuckin' kids then and I don't want them now."

Shaking my head side to side I said, "I should have a say so in this too, you know."

"You fuckin' do. You got two choices. Get your tubes tied or I'll divorce your ass," he instructed, pouting like a two-year-old child as he stomped to the bathroom, refusing to hear anymore from me.

My mind told me he'd soften up in time, but his childless declaration made me very uneasy. I edged to my side of the bed with my back turned away from him as D's selfishness took over everything, including children. I couldn't imagine not having kids but the fear of D abandoning me began to set in. I turned to my faith as it fueled me to remain calm and stay strong in my convictions.

Returning from the bathroom, he approached my side of the bed. In the dark, I could make out his outline hovering over me.

Agitated, he continued arguing, "if you want this damn marriage to work, you'll get your tubes tied or else I'm getting me a fuckin' lawyer."

The words pierced that place in a woman's heart that throbs for maternity. I struggled to not lash out at him. I attempted one last time to get D to look at things from a woman's perspective.

"It's not like we have to have kids right away. Maybe in a few years—even five if that would change your mind," I said, trying to reason as I began to beg, tears pooling.

But he refused to back away, demanding my full attention. D's temper could flare within seconds with or without alcohol and he was approaching an explosion. Although he had showered earlier, his body odor reeked of booze as it oozed from his skin. I found myself trying to soften the tone of our argument, but somehow I knew it was already a done deal. Irritated and getting madder by the minute, he blew.

"NO. I said FUCKIN' NO. I told you a long time ago we ain't having kids," he shouted.

I clammed up, too distraught to comprehend his demand. I couldn't imagine my life any emptier. Surely children would fill a void. I needed and wanted to feel love, appreciation, and most of all, I wanted a purpose other than being D's servant.

"The fuckin' decision is up to you."

Why would I want kids with that selfish bastard, I asked myself, fuming.

With years of perspective and now able to see the pattern that developed, the matter of his claiming that we had spoken about not having children was an early example of his gaslighting technique, designed to make me doubt myself. He often did things to make me think I was imagining things or had said things that I didn't. This took his cunning to a whole new level.

"I said you're getting your tubes tied or else divorce. I can't afford kids. Christ, you don't even have a god damn job yet and you want fuckin' kids," he screamed. "And just who in the hell is going to pay for all this shit?"

I wondered how other couples made it work. It wasn't like we were dirt poor. We certainly could afford muscle cars and everything else D wanted. His materialistic desires to possess things overrode my desire to have a family.

I had to accept the choice D gave me. I would submit, or divorce was inevitable. I refused to argue anymore as I shut my eyes, pretending he wasn't standing over me. But he switched on the bedroom light to get my full attention.

"Open your damn eyes and look at me. You make a doctor's appointment tomorrow and get yourself fixed. You fuckin' hear me?" he said, through bared, clenched front teeth.

I swallowed hard as I remained still.

Grabbing my forearm, he repeated, "Did you hear me?"

"Yeah ok," I said, as I tried to shake his grip that left a bruise on my arm.

That marked the beginning of a history of physical aggression. My submission pacified D. He smirked and slithered under the covers. But he wasn't done blindsiding me.

"And while you're at it, you need to see another doctor," he said.

"What do you mean another doctor . . . for what?" I said.

"Well, now that I'm your husband, you got to give it to me whenever I want it."

My eyebrows arched higher than they could be penciled. Like he didn't already 'get it enough,' my brain screamed.

"There's something wrong with you. You should be putting out more. You need to see a special kind of doctor for that, so they can give you some medication to fix your problem."

"What do you mean?" I asked, dumbfounded by yet another demand.

I was challenging his husbandly orders again and he didn't appreciate it.

"Fuckin' back talking me, are you?"

"No, I'm just asking you what you mean," I whispered as I held back tears, refusing to let him see me cry.

"You know what your fuckin' problem is? You are never in the fuckin' mood. There is something really fucked up with you," he spouted, degrading me. "Now that I'm your husband, I'm supposed to get it whenever I want it without fuckin' back talk."

D had no threshold of consideration for me. He didn't consider me anything other than property he owned. But then, I did nothing to help myself. Rather, I became the enabler that encouraged his bad behavior of childish temper tantrums and verbal abuse. We weren't friends or lovers, we just were. I said nothing, feeling worthless, but mad at myself for the mess I had created of my life.

As instructed, I made the necessary phone calls to become permanently motherless as my days grayed. It felt like mourning the death of a child in advance. I tried hard to lean on my faith but even that was getting harder as I felt abandoned. Shame, guilt, and regret were sucking me under.

The dreaded day arrived. At 5:00 a.m. I dragged myself into the passenger seat of the car.

I got a strange feeling that D was driving me to some remote place never to be found and somehow, I didn't care. Hugging my purse to my lap, pondering my decision, I tried to console myself with the thought that I was doing what I had to do to escape divorce court. I told myself God would understand and if judgment were to be passed, surely D would pay the price before me.

We headed toward the hospital in Duly. It couldn't be any easier for D to drop me off and pick me up as the hospital was conveniently located near his worksite. My stomach churned as we reached the hospital and my fate was becoming sealed.

"I'll pick you up around 3:30 right here, so be ready," he commanded. I could tell he felt awkward and didn't know what to say, so instead he continued to keep up his ranting attitude like he was still mad at me.

I had dreamed that D would come to his senses in a last-minute stay of execution. I paused, hoping he would say something anything. But nothing came.

"Yeah," I answered as I grabbed my crammed purse, and forced my shaking hand onto the handle of the door. I exited the car in slow motion and turned to watch D drive off. Even a dog would have been accompanied inside to be spayed.

Struggling to hold it together, I walked into the void, telling myself I'd get through it even though it was for him, not me. The elevator door opened, and I took in a deep breath before entering. Tears dripped from my nose as my head slumped to my chest.

I laid on the gurney before being put under, realizing that I had surrendered myself to D, bitter at the fact that he wasn't the one submitting to surgery or even holding my hand for reassurance.

With contempt in my heart, I fought the anesthesia that pitched me into darkness and childlessness at the age of 31.

6

Barren

UNDER THE ANESTHESIA I WAS in and out of consciousness in the recovery room. I began to gag and vomit as a nurse slid a small plastic pan to my mouth to catch what little contents were in my stomach.

"Kate, you're in the recovery room now," the nurse said in soft voice. "You'll be okay. Your body is reacting from the anesthesia."

I drifted back to sleep. Eventually I was taken back to a hospital room, where I dozed on and off, dry heaving a few more times.

Then, someone called my name again.

Forcing my heavy eyes opened, I squinted to steady the spinning room, in search of the voice.

Someone grabbed my forearm, shaking it hard.

"KATE, wake up," I heard.

My eyelids fluttered open as my ears echoed my name again.

"Come on. Get up, dear." The angry tone told me it had to be D. In my foggy state I realized D only called me "dear" in front of people. I flinched awake.

"I've been waiting for a half hour and it's after four. Why in the hell aren't you dressed," spouted D. "Get out of bed. We got to get going."

D brought me back to the harsh reality that I'd be going home to him and his strict regimen.

He yanked back the covers as if to pry me awake.

Sleepy-eyed and weak, I murmured, "I don't feel good D. I've been throwing up a lot."

"Well, you can throw up at home. Time to go," he argued back.

I wondered where the nurse was and how long he had been standing there attempting to rouse me. I tried to drag myself off the bed but was too groggy and unsteady to even pick up the ice water and get the straw to my mouth.

Just then a nurse entered. "We're going to keep your wife overnight until we can get her vomiting under control," she said to D, who looked very unhappy with the order.

I knew he would take his frustration out on me later for this. I drifted back to sleep for several minutes. The fact that a wrench had been thrown into D's well-organized plan chapped his ass. He intended to take me home and resume his life as if nothing had happened and the subject of children would be forever buried, never to interrupt his carefree life again.

The next afternoon I called D when I was told I could leave. D showed up again to retrieve me and this time, with the nurse in the room, D's mood morphed. He smiled at the nurse and then eyed my pale face, politely asking me how I was feeling. I wanted to vomit all over him, but I played along, replying that I was ready to go home. The nurse explained to D it was hospital policy to wheel patients out the door to a waiting vehicle. As we drove away, D bitched and moaned about hospital policy. Then I got an ass-chewing over the inconvenience of my ordeal. The tirade continued all the way home from the hospital. I laid my head against the head rest, agreeing with every word to minimize his temper. Before we reached home, D demanded that I get that day out of my system and never talk about it again.

I was ashamed I had agreed to his terms. He had succeeded in threatening me into submission and I had to keep it a secret. How does a newly married couple explain such a thing to a big Catholic family?

Several years later, D's six-year-old niece caught me off guard when she asked me why I didn't have kids like everybody else. I wondered if D's sisters had put her up to asking the question. I answered by saying that I didn't have all the right woman parts to make a baby. With that, she nodded like she accepted the answer. I would learn years later D told others that the reason we didn't have kids was because I suffered from severe endometriosis. I found it strange that he even knew the word 'endometriosis' and I realized he must have looked it up to formulate an acceptable excuse. Nevertheless, I continued the charade, covering his lies. After all, I did agree to it, plus, our marital problems were strictly ours.

As the baby blues continued, I slept often to escape. Those blues morphed into homesick blues for family and friends, ties of which had been all but severed by D, unbeknownst to me.

Shortly after our baby secrets were well buried, D located a red '80s corvette locally owned that he was interested in purchasing. He insisted that I go with him as if his potential purchase would delight me too, and we sped to the next town to check it out. His eyes bought it as soon as he saw the red shine. Days later, he revved the fancy engine all the way home while I followed.

I continued repressing my emotions, crying in secrecy and upping my nicotine highs with cigarettes. I was ashamed of how much I despised my husband of barely a year. Our marriage was a sham. I hated myself for marrying someone I couldn't stand and shaded my face with sunglasses to hide my swollen eyes.

To everyone but me, our marriage seemed natural and normal.

7

Grief

D'S TENDENCY TOWARD PHYSICAL DOMINATION continued after my hospital stay. One day, impatient with my slow emotional recovery, D cornered me in the kitchen.

"What's your fuckin' problem now?" Approaching any situation or argument, he always asked what my "fuckin' problem" was, throwing the entire blame on me as if I was the one that caused all our arguments.

I burst into tears as the weight of my awful decision to listen to D came to bear in that very moment. "I'll never be able to have kids because I did what you wanted not what I wanted," I blurted, no longer caring how angry it might make him.

"Are you fuckin' kidding me?" he said.

"We never discuss anything and make a joint decision because you make up your mind beforehand and what you say rules," I sobbed.

Trying to diffuse what I said, D repeated the old adage that I had heard him orate to others often. "You can't miss something that you never had in the first place and that includes fuckin' kids."

D did not have it in him to empathize. He just wanted me to 'get over it.'

"I'm sick of all this crying shit. Ain't nobody's fault but your own. You did it to yourself," he snared, trying to deflect blame from himself.

My mouth dropped from his audacity to throw it back in my face and turn it into my fault. "What?" I questioned, shocked by his heartlessness. If I had had a gun in my hand, I would have repaid him in kind, aiming below the belt.

"You heard me. It's your own damn fault cause you're the one who wanted to get your tubes tied," he shot back. My eyes widened as my body instinctively lurched toward him, and my front foot stomped the floor with a loud bang.

"No, I didn't. You threatened to divorce me if I didn't get my tubes tied," I said, spitting words.

"Nope, that's not what I said. What I said was that umm," he stalled to butter his lie with detail. Turning up the volume and fighting mad, I cut him off.

"That's a damn lie and you know it. You specifically said, 'me or divorce,' because you said you didn't want any fuckin' kids," I screamed back with air quotes for the last two words.

"Well, I didn't twist your damn arm to do it now, did I?" D shouted, maximizing his lie.

"I wanted kids," I squawked, crying uncontrollably as the past tense sound of that statement came to bear. "But you took that away from me."

"Then why in the hell did you get yourself fixed?" D questioned, grinning self-righteously, getting off on his power.

There was no point of arguing any further as he refused to take ownership, spinning it all on me. A nasty phlegm swarmed in the back of my throat, just begging to be hurled in his face as I gave myself permission to hate him more than ever. I had never felt so much hatred toward anyone, hoping he'd burn on earth before he burned in hell.

The fact that I had called him out made him more combative. Staring intensely, he walked me up against the kitchen doorway, his index finger stabbing at my chest.

"You'd better keep your fuckin' mouth shut and never bring this up again," he threatened. "It ain't nobody's fuckin' business what goes on in this house." His hands gripped the front of my T-shirt, twisting it in a ball. He slammed my back against the doorframe.

"Did you fuckin' hear me?" he said, showing all of his teeth. "You agreed to stay married instead of divorcing. I didn't fuckin' force you to do it. And now, it's a done deal, so shut the fuck up."

Too scared to open my mouth, I bobbed my head. In survival mode, I suppressed my fury. I was losing a piece of myself with every command. This was not me. This was D turning me into someone I hated, yet I couldn't help myself.

Our hideous marriage carried on each day. To others, it appeared as if we were a regular normal couple while absolutely no one knew our true existence.

Navigating my way through a marriage that felt unhinged became a way of life. Within a year's time, I had morphed from an independent single gal with hope for a bright future into a beaten down housewife with no future. D had learned that I would cower every time and it had the effect of pumping his ego even more. I wondered how much more inflated he could be if I never pushed back to stop his trajectory, yet to do so would be dangerous and foolish.

Like an obedient dog, I learned to bow to my husband's supremacy; sit on command, speak when spoken to, and shut up when told. Controlling me seemed very gratifying to D. The more I backed down from his condescending remarks, the more he plunged forward, building his ego and making me a slave to his every command. I learned not to dignify his insults with any answer, for it would only give him another excuse to assert his superiority. My demeanor became quiet as fear drove me to housewife him, not love him. I had become a full-blown addict to his abuse.

Whore Money

IN OUR SECOND YEAR OF marriage, I was becoming accustomed to D's daily militaristic routine. Bedtime was 7:00 p.m. to accommodate his 4:00 a.m. work schedule. I was expected to maintain the same schedule.

One night, I slid under the sheets and rolled onto my side as D shuffled from the bathroom. The mattress shifted as he scooted his butt onto the bed, climbing out of his boxers. I habitually kept as close to the edge of the bed as possible to avoid further contact.

"You ready?" he asked, laying on his back as he scratched his groin.

"For what?" I asked, stalling for time, too tired to go through the motions.

"Come on. You know what for."

"No. I don't."

Waving his hand toward my waist, he instructed, "Get over here."

"Nah, I'm too tired."

"Tired from what? I'm the one who worked his damn ass off all day." he said, fisting his hand and pounding his chest with it. "What the fuck did you do all day to get so goddamn tired?"

Unwilling to engage him, I didn't answer.

Continuing on, he scowled louder. "You're my wife and that means that I'm supposed to get it whenever I want it."

I wrinkled my nose, staring at his sprawled naked body, erected toward the ceiling.

"Geeze D, you just don't get it any time you want it," I said.

"I always got it before we were married and you never bitched and complained then." D never took 'no' for an answer.

"We're married now and that means anytime I want it, you're supposed to give it to me."

"Says who?" I protested.

"That's what fuckin' marriage is all about. I'm the boss," he barked back, pulling my arm toward his groin.

"That's not how it works," I said and pulled my arm away, trying to deescalate the situation.

"I'm your fuckin' husband and that means in the fuckin' bedroom too," he said, enraged.

Instantly, his huge hand reached for my head, grabbing the back of my scalp, yanking my tensed neck toward his stony glare. With no time to react, I went catatonic so he couldn't further move me. His jaw tightened and neck veins popped as he took ownership of me.

With a fistful of my hair locked in his fingers, D forced my face into his crotch. He had never had a penchant for oral sex and I was shocked by his sudden impulse.

"Stop it," I yelled, trying to get him to release his grip.

But D refused to back off.

Through my gritted teeth, I began to feel as if I was going to gag with the mere thought of it.

Apparently, the tussle was exciting to D as he consummated the act prematurely with my teeth still clenched. Instead, it exploded all over the side of my face and hair.

As the energy drained from his body and he released his grip, I sprang from the bed and raced to the kitchen gagging. As I wretched into the sink, I grabbed the bottle of dish washing soap and squirted the liquid all over my face to erase the nastiness and odor.

The next morning D was up earlier than usual getting dressed for work. His employment sent him to various job sites throughout the year as an equipment operator for heavy machinery. It was imperative for him to arrive early so as to gain possession of the keys to the company van. Co-workers riding the van were well aware of his unpredictable temper tantrums when he didn't get to drive the van himself. Most stepped aside to avoid conflict throughout the day's work schedule.

As D shuffled about to get ready, I dragged myself to the kitchen to prepare his lunch bucket for the day. Turning on the small TV to catch the local news, I noticed an exposed twenty-dollar bill tucked under D's billfold. Assuming he put it there to remind himself to gas the truck before he went off to work, I went about my morning routine. I never was allowed to access his billfold without permission. And I had always adhered to his commands.

I upped the TV volume and pulled the prepared sandwiches, cookies, chips, an apple and pudding along with several cans of caffeinated soda from the refrigerator shelves, meticulously packing them to fit around ice packs in his insulated lunch bucket. I had prided myself for packing a stuffed lunch box of goodies for D. But he never gave a compliment and the only way I knew whether or not he appreciated it was if he didn't complain.

Rinsing my hands in the kitchen sink, I thought of the night before and it instantly made me feel as if I was going to gag again. D entered the kitchen and sat on a kitchen chair putting on his work boots. I didn't bother to say good morning to him.

"There's a twenty on the counter," he said.

I turned sideways, wondering why he was telling me that.

"I thought you'd like some extra spending money."

Stunned, I said nothing to his contrived niceness. D had never given me extra money. In fact, it was just the opposite. I had to beg for money. It was obvious his conscience was paying me for last night's vicious attack. I thought I had compartmentalized my loathing but the smoldering rage almost escaped my pursed lips. My mind couldn't understand D's twisted thought process. For all the things D had forced and done to me, there had never been even the least bit of an apology. Now, money was supposed to fix everything. That twenty-dollar bill was prostitution money. At least that's what I understood from my pimp's breath-of-fresh-air conversation. I bit hard to hold my tongue. My eyes focused on the floor as I reached for the whore payoff and took the twenty.

"That enough?" he asked, knowing I wouldn't comment.

I responded with a nod. In his warped reality, he didn't get that his uncivilized way of having sex was nothing short of barbaric. For 11 years of dating, I allowed him access to my body begrudgingly, but oral sex wasn't part of the equation. In fact, neither of us ever brought the subject up. It seemed now his uncouth behavior was getting worse. I loathed myself as I scrunched the twenty into an angry ball of resentment and shoved it into my bathrobe pocket.

We never spoke of that night again. To satisfy D, I laid for him nearly every night for months and it became routine for him to leave money for me. There wasn't a payoff every time, and he got stingier with his money, lowering the payment from twenty to ten down to five. Occasionally, he would passive-aggressively punish me by withholding my whore money. This usually followed a night of sex in which D wasn't satisfied.

Indirect punishment also involved being grounded. If D wasn't in a good mood, I wasn't allowed to drive the car or make phone calls. He would determine what I would do for the day and would pack my hours with home chores.

I continued each day pretending nothing happened as I stared in the mirror, finding no happiness in my face. Feeling damned and worthless, there was nothing I could do about it but endure his ownership of me for nothing would change, or so I thought.

9

Dispatcher

SUNTON, POPULATION 1200, WAS A town one-fifth the size of Manley where I had last resided. It had a gas station, convenience store, grocery store, and three taverns, one of which was the Sunton Bar where D and I had gone on our first date and every weekend for years after. Other than rowdy bars, not much excitement happened in Sunton, but it had a dispatch center in the light plant that served emergencies for several surrounding towns and was the hotbed of excitement in Sunton. One day, D found out that the center needed a dispatcher. He had been pushing me to get a job since I had lost my previous job eight months earlier.

When I went to apply for the job, I quickly learned what a small-town mentality Sunton had. The good old boys that ran it had been in place forever and judging by their guts it looked like they weren't motivated to change a thing. The office was gloomy and smelled like 40 years of sweaty men smoking. I accepted the position with apprehension after D decided it was perfect for me. I looked forward to the prospect of earning my own money in a legitimate way.

I started work in the gloomy office with no formal training as they expected me to absorb what I needed to know. Aside from the struggle to figure things out,

I found myself cleaning constantly because I couldn't stand the filth and squalor that was our office.

Fire and ambulance calls were jotted on a piece of scratch paper and stuck on a small wooden block with a large nail protruding from the middle. It was located on a counter for all eyes to see, including anyone who walked through the door. When I complained about this, my complaint fell on deaf ears. Bar flies were regulars, stopping by under the auspices of wanting to say hello and would hang out at the counter to eye the nail block for good gossip to spread.

Within two years, I could tell my job was in jeopardy as I was clashing with too many of the good old boys who didn't like the changes I was making to the office. I heard through a friend that another friend of hers believed there was hanky-panky going on in the center as well. There definitely wasn't infidelity at the dispatch center, contrary to gossip. However, one elderly spouse, overly jealous of my office friendly conversations with her husband, caused quite a ruckus one day. After threatening her husband with a large kitchen knife, for which he called the police, she then threatened to come after me. She never did, but the drama made me look bad.

As I struggled to hold on to my job, I found out one day that confidential information that I had shared with my husband was getting leaked. One day, while visiting D's mother, she inadvertently referred to a story that I had told D in confidence. She couldn't have gotten it from anyone else because I hadn't told anyone else. D loved to be the purveyor of information because it made him feel important and I became concerned D was sharing that information with others as well. Although D had come to enjoy his newfound status as town crier on all things emergency by way of me, he didn't realize it was jeopardizing the very job he was enjoying at my expense.

After two and a half years, I was terminated on the grounds that I was incompetent at running the police and emergency radios. All the drama of my alleged affair with an obese old man with terrible halitosis didn't help. Neither did the fact that leaks of confidential information, probably stemming from D, were blamed on me. Though I had my supporters, including the fire chief, it didn't matter. D was pissed. D had held the same job forever and couldn't understand why I couldn't hold on to one for more than a few years. Plus, there went his source of town gossip and his name was publicly shamed by his incompetent wife, again.

"If Kate would've kept her fuckin' mouth shut, she'd still have a job," he said frequently, blaming me as he stretched the truth for drama.

With D fueling my fury toward city government, I felt bitter resentment, but it was a time when women were treated with disrespect, a place where hillbilly mentality ruled, and men were kings. With D goading me all the while, I began looking for another job, hiding my miserable employment rap-sheet with sarcasm and smiles.

10

D's Castle

IN THE SUMMER OF 1990, back in the prison of our house for entire days again. I had plenty of time to contemplate my incompetence, mulling my firing and the damage to my reputation, my stupid marriage, and my dead-end life. With every "worthless" comment leveled by D, my self-esteem declined. I knew that I had to get another job or rot in the house that was a shrine to D. I knew I'd never get a job in Sunton again as the entire town knew I had been fired, so I would have to look for work in other nearby towns. This further irritated D because I would have to spend more in gas and run up the odometer.

With employment uncertain for me, D began nagging me to cut back on everything. I wondered how I was supposed to cut back when I didn't spend on much of anything other than groceries and coin items at garage sales.

Twice a month D would anxiously await my unemployment checks. I had specific instructions to lay the full amount on the counter after cashing my checks. After counting the money, he would leave an allowance for what he felt I deserved. Sometimes, if he felt that the sex was good the night before, he would give me a raise.

To cope, and never having mastered alcohol consumption, I upped my cigarette habit. I had tried numerous times to quit over the years because D no longer smoked and didn't like it, but I was addicted. Despite D's hounding me, smoking seemed to be the one and only thing I could control, the one thing that left me feeling euphoric if even if for only for a few minutes and I wasn't about to give it up at that time. Because D was scrutinizing every penny I was spending, cigarettes became an issue. After one of his lectures on smoking, in a panic that D would deny me my one vice too, I stood up for myself and threw it in his face.

"I'll stop smoking when you stop drinking," I smarted back.

"Ahh fuck you," he said. "At least I have a fuckin' job that pays for my beer. I'm not paying for any more of your goddamn cigarettes."

Somehow, I would scrounge the money to buy a pack, bum from my neighbors, or sell some of my garage sale finds. I had convinced myself that cigarettes were responsible for getting me through each day.

Months dragged by and finally I landed a job at a toy factory in a small town 45 minutes from Sunton. What started out as a temporary summer job ended up as full-time employment months later. I was shuffled through the new plant as well as the old foundry performing different factory positions on assembly lines where needed. Repetitive motion became the number one health concern, yet the company turned a blind eye to serious claims, all the while touting their safety records. Work was physically exhausting and grueling hours contributed to low morale. Foreman and supervisors disrespected line workers, adding to the atmosphere of a prison-like workplace.

Eventually the repetitive motion on the line took its toll. I developed severe carpal tunnel in both wrists. I struggled for months to keep up. The company refused to admit job-related injury. Finally, I needed surgery on both hands. The surgery was only partly successful and I never regained full use or full feeling of my hands. According to the doctor, I suffered permanent nerve damage from waiting too long to schedule the surgery.

Aside from my hands, recovery from the surgery was slow for other reasons. I began to develop aching muscles and fatigue, along with balance problems. The doctors weren't sure why at first.

Because I had taken more medical days off of work than I had officially worked, I was fired as a result. D was more disgusted than ever, as it was another black mark on his reputation. He refused to accept my health problems, writing them off as 'all in my head.' He accused me of being lazy. I would hear from relatives and friends much later that he would rant about me saying, "Nothing wrong with her except she's fuckin' lazy and don't want to work."

Aside from the fact that I was no longer bringing in money, D had a new reason to feel contempt for me over my loss of the job. He would lose out one of my employee benefits that he had come to enjoy. I received a discount on toys. D had taken advantage of this and started to collect toy tractors and coin banks. It became an obsession. Each Friday he would instruct me to make a special trip to the toy outlet after work, to purchase discounted toys. He would send me with the exact change to purchase items he would circle in the company's catalog. I obeyed his orders, toting home boxes and cases of toys every week. D began buying floor-to-ceiling shelves as the collection began to fill entire rooms of our house. Eventually, four bedrooms, two hallways, and the attic of our home would be devoted to D's collection.

To justify his obsession with his toys, D would tell people that as a child he had never had toys and that since he worked damned hard for his money, he felt he deserved to spoil himself. It was a good story and worked well as far as tugging heart strings. He became consumed with his hobby and frequented toy stores, got involved in e-Bay bidding, and would send me to buy at auctions. He was happy to give me the car keys for such trips and gas money flowed easily from his wallet. I purchased new toys each week until I was terminated from the company due to my carpel tunnel.

D continued to collect even though he no longer got good deals from my discount, because he had learned that showboating his toy collection made him feel popular among co-workers, family, and friends.

His collecting hobby branched out to include other things like airplane models, beer mugs, football bowl mirrors, Coke products, and beer memorabilia. You could barely tell I lived in our house.

Even family pictures were eliminated to make room. D added a large cement block room onto the side of the garage to house over fifty die cast riding tractors and pedal cars, filling it to capacity.

The doctor appointments to Iowa City and Mayo Clinic looking for answers as to why I hadn't fully recovered from the carpal tunnel surgeries turned up a diagnosis of Fibromyalgia. This explained my widespread muscle pain, faltering balance, and extreme fatigue. Symptoms mimicking Multiple

Sclerosis made it difficult to diagnose. It was a devastating blow and a specialist informed me I needed to find work that did not require steady hands.

D had a field day impersonating my awkward movements, telling people that I was inebriated. He often kidded to others when I would lose my balance that I had come out as a closet drunk. Instead of defending myself, I held back, joking along with him and never making a scene in front of others. But alone, I spat back one day.

"I've never been drunk in my life and you know it," I said, feeling hurt by the joke.

"Yeah, well you know that, and I know that, but nobody else does, and people will believe me," he smirked. Everyone but those who knew me well believed every scheming lie D told.

Between hiding secrets, the humiliation of several job terminations, and hand surgeries, the depression and stress wreaked havoc on my body. I had become a tearful mess with no support from anyone. Throughout it all, D refused to accompany me to the many hospital visits I had, as he said he couldn't take off work, claiming he had no vacation days to use. I shuttled myself with much difficulty.

I took medication after medication to control muscle spasms, aching joints, severe headaches, flu like symptoms, and the sensitive pressure points that refused desensitization. Sleep deprivation made me dizzy, and when I would feel off balance, I would get nauseous.

I was embarrassed that I had to apply for disability benefits as demanded and ordered by D. After several rejection letters from the Social Security Disability Claims Department, we hired an attorney to fight for me. Weeks lengthened to months sending medical records and critical information documented from doctors and specialists as I awaited my fate. I heard nothing but money complaints from D. Our bank accounts, especially savings and CDs, were improving rather than diminishing, but he saw fit to complain and ride me about it. He was becoming meaner and more aggressive. We were barely on speaking terms, but I continued to cater to his whining and complaining.

When I did finally receive government disability benefits, D swore me to secrecy about it. He said receiving disability checks was as disgraceful as receiving welfare and he made me promise to tell no one, threatening me with vulgar language and jabbing a finger into my chest. I agreed.

When the disability checks began to flow, we went through the same routine where D would give me an allowance of what he thought I was worth.

I considered myself lucky to get what I got, never complaining it wasn't enough, because complaining would have given D satisfaction. Since I didn't grumble after he took more and more from my dwindling check, he continued to withhold more and more, seeking my limit. I refused to cave, and barely made ends meet. I had cooked, cleaned, washed his pissed bedsheets, stomached his disgusting vulgarity, kissed his ass, and dogged as his bitch in bed, but I'd be damned if I would beg for money that was mine in the first place. Though it was my money, he had first dibs on controlling how it was spent and where it would be safely kept—away from me.

After a while, D put me on a regular allowance.

I found out much later that D had been telling others I was high maintenance, and that he would have to work forever. Because I always did my best to look nice by way of garage sale bargains on clothing and because we lived in a nice house, no one would have guessed that my life subsisted at a poverty level.

By the time I was 36 in 1991, D had me completely dependent upon him for everything. I convinced myself there was no way I could survive on my own. I had to forget dreaming and maintain lucidity as D tested my sanity with his ego, and his maniacal system of secrets and lies designed to control my destiny.

11

S THE '90S WORE ON, our lives were a simple matter of patterns and
habits. As long as nothing out of the ordinary happened, D's ire would
stay at bay. I operated with military precision to keep everything in its
place, to make meals at the same time each day, and to go to bed when D was
ready. Routine was vital to his temperament. I hated holidays when new forces
would wreak havoc on our routine.

As my life narrowed, I became more secluded. Though I would stay busy all
day with a host of daily assignments from D, loneliness set in. I found myself
spying on neighbors for entertainment.

One day, in the summer of 1997, I noticed a middle-aged couple moving into
a ranch-style house that had been for sale just around the corner from our house.
I felt like a voyeur watching their every move as they settled into their new surroundings. To play it cool, I waited a few weeks before introducing myself. I had
to hide my excitement so I wouldn't look desperate.

Ellie and her husband, Kurt, became an asset to our neighborhood, taking pride in their property, staining their deck, primping their lawn, growing
a vegetable garden, and installing a small fountain under a shaded oak tree

in their backyard. They were friendly, down-to-earth folks whose fun-loving company was contagious.

I became fast friends with Ellie. She worked as a healthcare provider in the afternoons and she and I began taking walks together on nice mornings. My relationship with Ellie continued to flourish as months passed. When in the presence of Ellie, D would be pleasant and encouraging of our friendship, insisting that we have nice walks, but when alone with D, I began to sense that my brighter disposition and how straight I was standing was irritating him. He began questioning where we would walk, how long the walks were, and what we discussed. He became increasingly agitated with the friendship and was taking it out on me in passive-aggressive ways, picking fights with me after phone conversations with Ellie, or if I didn't feed him enough details about our walks.

Eventually, D introduced himself to Ellie's husband. They began buddying up to each other with open-garage chats and this seemed to make D relax about Ellie. Aside from relief, I was happy that we had found a couple that we both seemed to like. I imagined the four of us getting together to play cards or have barbeques. But on our walks, Ellie began to disclose what Kurt relayed to her about his conversations with D. Aside from getting details about our walks and talks, D was belittling me and calling me lazy and worthless.

The many times Ellie and I got together, I never mentioned my health problems affiliated with Fibromyalgia. D had drilled it into my head that no one wanted to hear me complain about my so-called 'imaginary' symptoms. One day, Ellie asked me how I was doing, as if I had been sick. I laughed, stating that we're all getting older and it seemed aches and pains were ever-present, but generally speaking, I was okay.

A sick feeling washed over me as weeks earlier I was asked the exact same question by another girlfriend who also knew D. Twice in a row was no coincidence. At the time, something seemed off, yet I dismissed it, thinking I was reading more into something that didn't exist.

I said that I didn't have cancer, asking her why she had asked. Ellie said that D had told them I suffered lots of health problems and wasn't doing well. Furthermore, D had told them that I was a closet drinker. This would serve as a good explanation for why I lost my balance on occasion.

That night I told D what Ellie had said.

"You know I don't drink," I said as the argument heated up.

"Yeah, well, you know it and I know it, but other people don't know it," he mocked.

I shook my head in disdain. I loathed that revolting hypocrite who owned me by a paper document called a marriage license, and wished it included an expiration date.

Stretching his arms wide he said, "Look around the house. All I see is wine bottles everywhere. Just proves my point now, doesn't it?"

"Those wine bottles are for decorations and you know it. Besides they've never been opened."

"Well, just proves my point once again," he laughed. "You got spare bottles stashed everywhere, just like an alcoholic," he said, taunting me further.

He was the nasty drunkard and now he was accusing me of the same exact thing.

"What did I ever do to you that you have to be so ornery and mean to me?" I leveled.

D just smirked.

I shut my mouth, jamming my middle fingers in midair as he turned around to walk off.

Over the years Kurt and Ellie's eyes opened to the true D. They began to see his resentment toward Ellie. I am convinced he envied my ability to get close to people and I think, in his heart, he wanted to be able to do the same, but he didn't know how. He couldn't be himself and be close to people at the same time. The two were not congruous. His relationships were superficial, or ended without explanation.

When his ploys to tarnish my image with Ellie and Kurt didn't work, D resorted to accusing Ellie and me of being lesbians, to drive a wedge between us. Add his drinking to the conversation and D would erupt with jealousy, ordering my ass to stay home, stop walking with Ellie and wandering the streets looking like two 'fuckin' whores.' Mortified by his accusations, I was ashamed to tell Ellie, knowing she would tell Kurt. So, I didn't. We kept walking.

$$\underline{12}$$

Fence

IN THE EARLY PART OF 2000, D's OCD peaked one hot humid summer day after he returned home from work in a foul mood. As usual, he took the brunt of his lousy day out on me and the kitchen counter top, slamming his lunch box on the counter.

"A bunch of fuckin' babies," he ranted.

I grabbed his lunch box and began unloading the contents. My eyes shifted side-to-side in trepidation. I stepped closer toward the refrigerator for space, maintaining silence around D's unpredictable temper.

"I should be getting paid double to babysit fuckin' kids," he grumbled.

D had zero tolerance for accepting others who weren't his caliber of perfection, especially newbie co-workers.

Minutes later, he sat at the kitchen table staring the small TV, flipping to the local news station. Taking his anger out on me, he complained of the ungodly heat in the kitchen, as if it was my fault.

"Yeah, I know," I replied, "I've got both fans set on high."

Slamming his beer can onto the tabletop he ordered, "Well, open a fuckin' window."

"But, if I open a window, I'll be letting all the humidity in . . ."

"I said, open a fuckin' window, NOW," he said as he sprang to his feet, pointing toward the window. He couldn't stand the word 'but.'

I apologized, pulling the dark shade upward. The old glass window frame rattled as I pushed up from the bottom and used a broken yardstick to prop it open. The humid air layered the kitchen, as sweat gathered on my brow. I had begged for years to have central air installed but D refused. He was too cheap to pay for central air. He seemed to enjoy watching me suffer in the heat as an equalizing payment for how much he suffered from lack of air conditioning at work.

We normally ate at 5:00 p.m. sharp per D's requirement. I tried to lighten his mood, asking if he was ready for supper.

"Hell no. I ain't done drinking my beers," he answered, staring at the TV screen.

My fingers fidgeted. Locking them in prayer appeased my anxiety from the heat. His bad moods meant punishment for me. It was how he released fury, by finding something for me to do that involved servitude. Immersing me in physical labor tickled his fancy.

"Tomorrow, I want you to get your fat ass outside and bleach the fence. All of it."

Turning sideways, I focused my eyes on D. I had never shied away from work, but I also knew my limitations and he did too. He was pushing the envelope just to see me sweat.

"Did you fuckin' hear me?" he snarled.

"Yeah," I said.

"You get your ass out there tomorrow morning bright and early. I got to get up early every fuckin' day for work and there ain't no reason why you can't do something besides sleep."

"Yeah, but um to-to-tomorrow," I stuttered.

"So, tomorrow you can get some exercise bleaching that fuckin' fence," cussed his gutter mouth. "Besides, you can fuckin' sleep when you're dead." That was one of D's brilliant sayings.

I chose to keep foul language to myself, muttering under my breath only, for I had no choice but to obey his orders if I didn't want to pay the consequences.

The next day, with a half-bucket of water and a gallon jug of bleach, I walked the fence line. As I finally landed on the pea rock that surrounded the fence line,

I smelled a foul odor. D routinely burned carcasses of animals that died from drinking the anti-freeze he'd deliberately set out just for them. The odor smelled like burning hair. I dropped the bucket handle and decided to investigate the atrocious smell.

My nose led me to the smoldering burn barrel that we used to burn garbage and brush. I wondered what D had burned this time. I pinched my nostrils as I moved closer. I almost lost my stomach contents as I started to gag. With my other hand, I lifted the screened lid to discover partial remains of several cats. Burnt fur, bones, and skeleton heads still smoldered as I slid the lid back over the top of the barrel.

Backing away, my agitated stomach churned as vomit spewed from my mouth. Already dehydrated from the heat, I became dizzy as I wiped the sourness from my lips. D had talked about killing stray cats to cure their pissing habits that blemished his meticulous lawn. But this was the first time I found evidence that it was true.

Too nauseated to withstand the heat and the smell, I never got the fence bleached that day. It took me a week, slow as I was and as hot as it was, of carrying half-buckets of water and gallons of bleach to accomplish the task for the garden hoses wouldn't reach the long distance to the fence. The combination of putrid smells, the chemical fumes, and the summer heat made me sick for weeks. My lungs felt raw and I coughed bloody phlegm. The coughing exacerbated my Fibromyalgia symptoms, causing my upper torso to spasm. Yet I refused to give him the satisfaction of hearing me complain.

The very last day, D re-examined my labors and angrily tromped into the house with beer can in hand. The higher he stepped, attempting to maintain balance, the greater the inebriation and I knew to be on my guard. I had learned that earlier in my life from my father's alcoholism.

"The fence is still fuckin' dirty," he belted.

I chewed the corner of my lower lip as I listened to him go on and on about each speck I missed from the fence posts to the railing.

As I stood there taking his crap, I wondered how far back in life D's wires got crossed and OCD took over. There was no sense arguing with him or his drunken fault finding. Nothing was ever good enough or clean enough for him.

I said nothing and took it. Usually, I apologized to keep the peace.

"You WILL get your ass out there tomorrow and go up and down the fence line, wiping every one of those fuckin' spots off."

I nodded my head yes and said, "fuck you" under my breath. Swearing at him gave me the tiniest bit of joy when joy was so hard to come by.

13

Escape

B Y LATE SUMMER OF 2003, the abuse went from verbal to physical, as things continued to deteriorate and my desire to leave him grew. But, as apparent as my discord was, it was also apparent that I would never be able to leave him because it wasn't in the realm of possibility. I was supposed to stay married, hope for the best, and put up with the worst.

Long holiday weekends meant the monotony of staying home with D. Labor Day weekend began the same as any other weekend. That Saturday morning I was making D's coffee as we passed in the kitchen without a word.

D proceeded outside to the porch with his coffee to survey his neighborhood land, before commencing his Saturday morning pomp and circumstance. It was a ritual that started with the opening of the roll-up-door, which was loud enough to become a familiar sound around the block on Saturdays. He would time it so the door opening revealed him in the act of sweeping the already immaculate garage. Next, he would set about to pull everything out of the garage as a grand display of his work ethic. It also made him look like the busier of the two of us. He would come back in the house and complain to me that so many people were stopping by that he couldn't get a thing done, exaggerating his heavy workload.

Labor Day Monday brought rain to the area as forecasted. Strong winds blew off a few shingles, and a leak sprung in the living room ceiling. Leaks were not a part of the routine. The surprise made D's demons spring into action with the first drip that hit the floor. The leak had occurred before in the same spot and D seemed most angry at the rain, swearing volumes at it.

Unable to stop the rain and unwilling to go on the roof until it quit, D plopped onto the reclining sofa, and started drinking early. He began clicking through the TV channels to find NASCAR races.

I was happy to stay in the kitchen as racing cars didn't interest me. I prepared hot ham and cheese sandwiches for his lunch and served it to him on the couch. I knew that hunger made him ornerier and I hoped his comfort food and cold beer would sooth the beast in him. I went back to the kitchen to stay out of his sight.

Minutes later he hollered, "I need another sandwich."

Harkening to his call, I jumped up and nuked another sandwich in the micro- wave, knifing it in half, as he liked it.

"And while you're up, run out to the garage, bring a six-pack and find room in the refrigerator," ordered D.

I headed out the porch door per his command.

D had been fairly decent to me that day until I quietly toted in a pile of used books and settled into the seat next to him. I had been to a garage sale the day before and purchased a stack of books for a quarter a piece. There was also a box of free books and I helped myself to a number of outdated college textbooks including psychology, literature, and sociology. I couldn't wait to explore them and because his car races, which I was expected to endure alongside him, bored me, I thought the perfect solution was to read something. Plus, I thought it might up my intelligence quotient, which D had convinced me was so lacking.

Never content to see me at leisure, and always in need of my locked-in atten- tion, the minute I opened a book, D ordered me to retrieve another beer. I did so and sat back down again, grabbing a book. He started in on me.

"I don't know why you read this fuckin' shit, you don't get any smarter."

Agitated I hadn't replied, he twisted sideways, yanking the book from my hands. I flinched, scared he was reaching for my throat.

"What did this shit cost?" he scorned.

"I got them at a garage sale," I answered.

"I don't give a flying fuck where you got them," he said. "You're stupid enough without reading this shit." Anytime I was content, he made a point to make sure it wouldn't be for long.

I stared at the TV screen for several minutes and then nonchalantly grabbed another book and opened the pages, ignoring him.

"Getting any smarter?" he mocked as he reached over and yanked another book from my hands, hurling it forward. The airborne book accidentally caught the corner of one of D's toy tractors, knocking it off the display shelf.

My body froze knowing the situation was about to get uglier, because sure enough, it was my fault that the book flew out of his hand.

"FUCK— look what you did," he yelled. "You just better pray that tractor doesn't have any fuckin' broken parts or else I'll," he caught himself from finishing criminal words as he stomped over to the toppled tractor, eyeing for damage.

Lucky for me, the carpet softened the tractor's blow. Constructed of die-cast, it was one of hundreds I had purchased while employed at the toy factory back in the early '90s. The melodrama continued.

Anger outlined his face as he delicately set the unharmed tractor back on the display case, his eyes on me like daggers. Panic gripped me as I struggled to make my legs move, knowing he was coming for me. But it was too late. With a full head of steam, he grabbed the front of my shirt, twisting to secure his grip on me and, yanking me off the couch, he hurled me against the wall. Like a fainting goat with inability brought on by fear, I froze in panic.

With his large hand embedded around my jaw, I could smell his sour breath as he shouted, "This is what I think of your fuckin' books," he said, as he spat in my face.

As veins on his neck ballooned, he twisted his fingers tighter around my jaw, constricting my breathing. I gasped for air.

"You're damn lucky I didn't break your fuckin' neck for that little stunt," he sneered, releasing his grip.

I limped forward as my weak knees tried to hold my legs steady. Rubbing my jaw, I gulped air, inhaling and exhaling to catch my breath.

"It's your own goddamn fault I get so fuckin' mad. You always got to cross the line," he said. "Now, clean this shit up," he commanded.

I trained my eyes on him as I pitched my books in the garbage. On the verge of exploding myself, I willed my hatred to simmer down by concentrating on a way to another life.

Just once I wished D would admit his meanness. His impulsiveness was intensifying, not just when he was high-stepping. I never knew when he would spring. Any little thing irritated him. Now books pushed his buttons.

I hibernated in the upstairs spare bedroom to wait out the rest of the day before he went to bed. Mentally exhausted, I conked out under the coverlet. I awoke a few hours later to the sound of the TV downstairs. I tiptoed down the steps to find D slobbering down a bowl of cereal. It was past suppertime and he had not bothered to order supper from me.

With work the next day, D's bedtime was precisely 7:00 p.m. I knew he would be retiring within minutes, and would take the tension with him. As soon as he finished his cereal, he dropped it in the sink for me to clean. Neither of us said anything. I was still fuming about the disposal of my books.

Books were my escape but he didn't want me to escape. He didn't want me smarter than him. He wanted to keep me from growing. To grow might mean to discover a world of possibilities that might not include him.

At 7:00 p.m. sharp, he retreated to the bedroom. I wasn't about to sleep with him that night. I plopped on the couch as soon as the bedroom door closed. I slowly upped the TV volume to prevent him from sleeping soundly, telling myself it was the least I could do for him, considering what he had done for me that afternoon.

"Turn that fuckin' TV down. Some of us have to work tomorrow," D yelled.

Muting the remote, I hollered back through the closed bedroom door, "I wanted to read a book, but you made me throw them in the trash. Now, I don't have anything to read. It's your fault I have to watch TV."

"Turn that fuckin' thing down or I'll cut the fuckin' cables."

I upped and downed the volume, toying with him.

"What? I can't hear you," I said.

He flung the bedroom door open, and stepping high in his bare briefs, he grabbed the remote that rested on the sofa cushion. He clicked the "off" button, shutting down the screen and screamed, "Crazy bitch," and returned to the bedroom, slamming the door.

I sat brooding as I stared at the blank TV screen. The thought popped into my head to check whether or not D had stashed enough money in the freezer door to pay for my escape. I imagined that I would need a week's worth of expenses until I could figure out what else to do.

I snuck into the kitchen and quietly pulled the freezer handle. Flipping the flexible Tupperware lid with trembling hands, I counted close to $1,000. That would more than suffice.

My mind raced as to what I should take. D could come out from the bedroom and stop my progress so I hurried along. Already in the kitchen, I began ransacking cupboards to save money on food.

I then snuck to the bedroom closet and grabbed an armful of clothes and shoes, stuffing them into a garbage bag. After collecting my toiletries and packing everything in the car, I returned to retrieve the car keys from the kitchen key hook.

Knowing D might still be awake, I yelled, "Go fuck yourself. I've had enough of your shit. I'm leaving."

"Ahhh I ain't worried. You'll be back," he said nonchalantly.

My memory of that night put my car north of Sunton as I took to the open highway. As my teeth chattered, my frame of mind continued to fog. I couldn't stop dwelling on what D had drummed into my brain over the years; that I couldn't make it on my own; that I was crazy; that I had no family, no friends, no job, that I was worthless. I felt as fucked up as he said I was. My bleak future was nothing without moral support. Still, I couldn't bring myself to break my silence. Maybe I hadn't hit my personal low yet. I thought I had hit the bottom, but obviously not. I wasn't yet ready to share secrets.

I knew no one was in charge of my happiness but me. I couldn't find happiness though and I was beginning to hate the world, God, and myself. I had to admit that when I was angry, I was at my weakest. He had me hating myself more than I hated him. I wasn't only at war with D, I was at war with myself.

I needed myself to need me more than D needed me—to like me enough to protect myself and find a way out. I was convinced I still had fight left in me as I had gotten this far. As my brother Lee used to say: it's not the size of the dog in the fight but the size of the fight in the dog. I had dreamed this day would come and I would be strong.

My dogged determination reminded me that just because I was married to D that didn't justify his brutality. I was convinced my ballsy move would boomerang and I would suffer the consequences. My purpose in life wasn't to just serve my abusive husband, I was sure I would find my purpose if I could just find a way out of my marriage.

I continued driving for miles with no clue where I was headed. Finally, I spotted a motel. Turning off the engine, I breathed a sigh of exhaustion as I tried to salvage myself. I went to the front desk to check in, leaving everything else in the car but my purse. After giving my license number and paying with D's loot, the clerk handed me a key to my safe room for the night.

I located my room, locked and chained the motel door, and plopped onto the double bed where I proceeded to pummel myself. Without money I won't survive. I was stupid to do this. My life sentence to D was my fate: I had made the wrong choices early in my life and I would have to pay.

As I laid there sobbing on the spring textured mattress, fear began to override my will. If only I had the guts to reveal my secrets to the right person, maybe I could get help. But I wasn't ready to commit to that extent. The fear gnawed at me all night as I tossed and turned on the miserable mattress. By the next morning as the sun rose, I knew that my conviction to be free had been an attempt in vain.

Head hanging, I drove back home to face the consequences. I wouldn't even try to fix our marriage any longer. By that point I knew it was hopeless. The best I could hope for was to live out my life upstairs with him downstairs.

14

Returning Home

I FELT DEFEATED AS I drug myself back to him and his habitual ways. I passed a car with a bumper sticker that reminded me of the cryptic sticker adhered to D's gun cabinet which read, "The one who dies with the most toys wins." Wins what? I used to think. It spoke volumes about how materialistic D was. While I wasn't one of his toys, I was certainly his possession.

As I pulled into the driveway, I knew I had to do something different because the more aggressive D got, the more cowardly I became. He knew I was a weakling and I knew I had to get out in front of this mess to prove to him I wasn't taking his abuse any longer.

I realized my mindset needed an overhaul. What I was doing wasn't working. The thought occurred to me that with D treating me as worthless and lazy, I should act worthless and lazy. I might as well give him something to complain about since he already was complaining. This would infuriate him, but I had to mix it up and do something new.

I made sure I was on the couch watching TV when D returned home that afternoon from work. Neither of us spoke. I upped the volume on the TV, keeping a tight grip on the remote. He switched on the kitchen TV full blast.

Several hours passed. Hungry, I decided to go to the kitchen. D was glued to the TV. His submissiveness told me he was feeling me out. We didn't speak a word. I busied myself making a sandwich, leaving a mess behind, and returning to the living room. When I finished eating my sandwich, I lit up a cigarette knowing it would further my cause of letting him know I had had enough, for I usually never smoked in the house unless I was really angry with him.

I found it quite comfortable living in a bubble, putting myself first as I idled on the couch. He'd never seen me detached like this but he remained passive.

The stalemate went on for days. I continued provoking leaving faucets dripping, cupboard doors wide open, and light switches on. When he didn't react, I upped the ante by leaving still smoldering, overflowing ashtrays. For added effect, I dropped potato chips to the floor, crushing them under my feet. I drank from every glass and cup, leaving them wherever my heart desired. I stopped flushing the bathroom toilet. I found revenge entertaining and creative. It was my only reprisal without destroying things.

All the while he remained aloof. He expected me to apologize as usual but I held out. He owed me an apology. He owed me a lifetime of apologies. I was certain he'd bribe me, allowing me use of the car for a day out. That was his way of luring me back under his dominance.

By day three, I could tell he was at wit's end. He was slamming things and mumbling obscenities to himself. After he had cleaned for several rigorous hours, he sauntered into the living room and sat next to me. Steepling fingers was a sign of confidence for D and I could tell he was still not ready to cave. I slipped the remote between myself and the recliner cushions for subliminal control as I continued to stare at the TV screen.

Finally, he broke.

"Ahh so how long is this going to go on?"

Crossing my arms, I spit words, "You tell me. You're the one who ruined Labor Day weekend by making me throw away my books, which you then blamed me for."

Seeing a bucky side to me, he didn't know what to say. He tried to change the direction of the argument.

"So, where did you go?"

His demeanor showed he knew that he had pushed me too far. This was the first time I had him seemingly contrite, but I kept my guard up. Though I had failed miserably in my bid to leave him, I was beginning to feel it made a difference in some small way. I had found a vulnerability in him. His fear of divorce made him realize that his money was at stake and nothing meant more to him than his money. I let him squirm a little, being aloof, hesitating to answer too soon. I wanted him to wonder where I had been. Trying to promote conversation, he kept his temper in check. He began to pace the floor to calm himself and then tried a softer approach.

"I appreciate you putting my money back in the freezer," he said, throwing me a bone.

My eyebrows arched, shocked by his calm, cool temperament. I knew he was groveling for my mercy because not one single vulgar word rumbled from his mouth.

"You know, if you didn't push my buttons, I wouldn't get so mad at you," he said. "If you could stop crossing the line, maybe we could get things back to normal." The blaming portion of the disguised apology had begun.

I came on fast and hard, throwing it back in his face.

"You tried to choke me to death," I yelled. "And I did nothing to deserve that. Where is all this hate coming from?"

We sat in silence as he refused to answer the question directly. He changed the subject.

"Is your Fibromyalgia acting up again? 'Cause you look awful?" he asked, pretending to care.

Tired and drained, I was well aware I looked like death warmed over, but I refused to speak.

"You know, you can't sleep on that couch forever. You got to come to bed sometime," D said, trying to persuade me using something that would benefit me, but it was tinged with begging.

Silence was my ticket in getting across to D that I meant business. Refusing to recognize his so-called compassion toward me, I slouched in the recliner, staring straight ahead. I had command of his control button, but he was a master at exploiting my weakness to make me want him and need him again. This time, it wasn't working. Next, he tried bribing me.

"You know, I need a few things at Menards and Sears. I'll let you take the car to Cedar Rapids shopping tomorrow. And when you go, I'll give you the money to get my stuff and whatever money is left over, you can have," he said.

Changing focus onto something else, he pointed to the worn sofa cushions.

"You know, I think it's time to get a new couch, don't you think?" he said. "Tomorrow morning stop in Manley and price sofas."

D prevented humiliation by not apologizing, yet coming across in his mind as if he did.

I glanced his way, wanting more than ever to believe his newfound generosity. Appealing to my domestic desperation made me cave and I nodded 'yes.' His ego instantly roared back to life.

"Now that we got this all settled, I'm going to bed. I'll see you in a little bit, cause you're coming to bed, aren't you?" he asked, expecting sex within the hour.

With D, everyone owed him a favor. And now he was collecting. I tried to deny him, but ended up giving in, appeasing him. We started all over again, doing the exact same thing to pretend marriage where there was none, with D in full control.

The next day, I priced new couches in Manley and traveled to Cedar Rapids, running errands for D. I had already anticipated having little money left over after buying D's list of must-haves. I returned from Cedar Rapids filled with excitement, anticipating a new couch in the next few days, upon D's approval, of course. But weeks and months turned to a year as D continuously made excuses for being unable to go with me to the furniture store to approve the couch. The sore subject came up again in December 2004.

15

Deaths in the Family

I N EARLY DECEMBER OF 2004, my oldest sister Evie called our home. She said our father had been hospitalized at the Manley Hospital, critically ill. Considering this was a family emergency, I assumed D would drop everything and we'd leave within seconds. Unfazed, he waved me off, saying he was too busy to go as he spit shined his snow blower.

Disgusted but not surprised by his insensitivity, I took the car without his permission. As I sped to the hospital, the pit in my stomach grew as I imagined the reality that my father could soon be gone. Aside from the average grief a person would feel knowing their father may die, my angst was complicated by the fact that I had never made up with my dad, and now it might be too late.

Some 30 years earlier, when I was in my late twenties, by which time my father had become a dangerous drunk, I found out he was driving drunk with kids and grandkids to the lake and taking them out on his motorboat. He had to be stopped and my brother Ronnie agreed with me. We went to the courthouse to ask for information and told the clerk of court about our father, his history of alcoholism, and how worried we were that he was driving drunk. The clerk informed us that we could force our father into rehab at the local hospital's "psych" center with two signatures from family members. The clerk provided paperwork and we signed our dad away.

That evening, when my father got home from the tavern, two policemen showed up to get him. Dad sat at the head of the kitchen table fuming and refusing to go. One of the cops had been a friend of his and I suspect they let him stay the night for that reason. They showed up the next morning again to haul him away. This time Dad went without resisting.

I felt terrible about it, but my guilt was compounded when I discovered that my other 10 siblings were furious that Ronnie and I had perpetrated this cruel act on our father. We were blindsided, having assumed they would thank us for being the ones to solve the problem. My father went through rehab and became sober for the rest of his life, and though he forgave Ronnie, he never forgave me, completely ignoring me every time he saw me from then on and refusing to come to my wedding a few years later. The whole situation created a rift between me and my family that may never go away.

By the time I arrived at the Manley Hospital, a medivac chopper had been called to transport my father to a better-equipped hospital, but before it arrived, my father had passed on from complications of emphysema. Estranged from my family all those years, I wasn't aware how close to death he had been.

Still angry at D, I had to let him know of my father's passing. This time, I assumed he would come right away. Because I didn't have a cell phone, I had to borrow one.

"D, dad died," I cried.

"Wow! He went fuckin' quick, didn't he?"

I dug deep to contain myself and asked him to meet me at my mother's house, where the rest of the family planned to converge.

"There ain't nothing to do at your mom's but feel sorry for yourself. Besides, I got things to do at home," he said.

"But D, couldn't you come just for a little while and then you can leave early if you want," I begged.

"I told you I ain't coming," he spouted back. "And since you're in Manley already, you can stop at the furniture store and order that damn couch that you thought you had to have."

"For God's sake, Dad just died. Does it have to be today, of all days?" I said, shaking my head in disgust.

"You order it today before you go to your mom's, 'cause otherwise, the store will be closed when you go home," he commanded.

"D, I said dad died and . . ."

Angrily, he interrupted. "You want that fuckin' couch, you order it today, or else forget it."

I was too devastated to do anything except what came naturally and that was to obey D's orders. I went to purchase the couch.

Days later, on the way to the wake, D complained of the demands funerals place on his attire. I reminded him that people show their respect by dressing to honor the deceased.

"He was a fuckin' drunk."

I was too stunned to reply as I gritted my teeth in anger.

"Just think of all your inheritance money he pissed away on booze."

I stared out the side window, wishing him dead instead of my dad. I craved sympathy from my husband, but D couldn't mourn because he couldn't feel. As I grieved by myself, I wondered how he would react when the time came to say goodbye to his mother when she passed on. I was sure it would be the complete opposite of the hell he was putting me through. I was sure he would demand all sorts of sympathy and would never put up with someone calling her names.

At the funeral home, D became antsy with nothing to do. He managed to persuade my brother-in-law to ditch the wake in favor of the local tavern. Knowing D could consume a considerable amount of alcohol within one hour, I assumed he was quite inebriated when he returned hours later to the funeral home. Red-faced and smirking happy, he swayed as he high-stepped into the room where my father's coffin rested. I struggled to hold my contempt in check, while I continued to greet people in the receiving line.

During the wake, my family had felt cold and indifferent to me and I began to wonder about the origin of the bitterness. We had gotten by the mess of my forcing my father into sobriety because in the end, everyone was happier for it, so I knew their cold shoulders did not stem from that. I struggled to make sense of the distance between us and began to wonder if D's mask of deception had infected them too.

For months after my father's funeral, I grieved for him. It was not so much the kind of grieving for something lost as it was for something wanted. While my family forgave me and moved on, my father never forgave me. I wanted my father to go to his grave loving me, not holding a grudge.

I got to the point where I couldn't bring up my father's name for D had told me he didn't want to hear me blubbering anymore. D had insisted that my father drank his life away. While it was true that my father had been a drinker, he had cleaned up his act decades before his passing, and I had gained a lot of the respect back. I mourned the times I didn't have—the times that D deprived me of going to see my dad. I was jealous of my family for the last happy years they got to spend with him. All the while, I was clueless that D had been systematically pitting me against my father and my father against me.

Life in our house went on as usual after losing my father. From freezing each other out with dead silence to screaming and yelling vulgarity from D's mouth, he continued blaming me for any fucked-up day. I continued cleaning, washing and preparing meals to D's inspection all the while hoping he'd choke on a chicken bone and put an end to my misery. I would climb that stairway to a new life.

For the next five years, we continued the marital charade of playing house as strolling neighbors stopped by to chat like we were as normal as them. Throughout the five years after my father's death, my mother slipped into depression and dementia. I was unaware of her health problems as well.

Klaver family life reunions were celebrated without me and D. In those five years, we attended only a few holiday celebrations with my family. D would mingle like a seasoned politician and I came across as the moody sister, mad at the world sitting by myself, hating my husband while he had my family in the palm of his hand.

Early in 2009, my mother passed away in a nursing home from complications of dementia. As I prepared myself for the next few days of family chaos, I knew I had to find the will to wear the same plastered mask as I did for my father's wake and funeral.

I, like my family, was all about the illusion of closeness—putting on the big show—pretending we were one big happy family.

My mother's funeral was much like my father's. I felt so depressed I hardly said anything to anyone and everyone treated me with indifference. After my mother's funeral, I moped around for days, but I knew to keep it from D, for he would only add to my sadness.

One afternoon, D happily informed me that we were having company within the hour. I momentarily rose from my slump.

"Who's coming," I asked.

"Your niece and her husband," he said with uncharacteristic delight.

"Which one?"

"Josie and Tanner."

"Why are they coming to see us?" I asked.

"They want to see my collection of farm toys."

I had hoped they were coming to reminisce about good times with my mother, Josie's grandmother, but D had taken advantage of networking opportunities at the wake, to brag about his toy collection and my niece and her husband got roped into a tour of his greatness.

"Why did you need to invite them today?" I asked.

"Oh, I didn't. They invited themselves."

"Really!"

"Yeah, really," he said.

In that moment, I was certain that they hadn't invited themselves but rather, D needed his high, his fix, achieved by showing his toy collection. Who better to target and impress than the young who are vulnerable and gullible to his deception. And my niece and her husband were perfect subjects.

I shook my head, wishing Josie and Tanner would visit another day.

"What's your fuckin' problem now?"

"Nothing," I said, thinking I'd have to plaster a smile on my face when they came.

"Geeze, I thought you'd be happy to have your family visit you."

"I am. It's just not a good time. And besides, they're coming for you, not me."

"Christ, one minute you complain you don't get to see your fuckin' family. And the next, you're bitching and complaining when they do come to visit. Which one is it?" he barked. "Cause you can't have it both ways."

Tears flooded my eyes as I stood there and took his vulgarity. D noticed I was crying and tried to apologize in his own twisted way.

"I don't like to yell at you but, goddammit Kate, you need fuckin' help. You need a damn psychiatrist. You're not thinking straight. Your memory is shot," he listed. "You hate everyone around you and you take it out on me. And I'm fuckin' sick and tired of this bullshit."

I clenched my teeth to keep from telling him he was the lunatic who twisted everything I said and did it to make me look crazy. And he was telling me I needed help. As I fought to silence my hatred for him, I wondered if his heart could get any colder.

As I continued to grieve the loss of both parents, inheritance money was the last thing on my mind but the first on D's. He couldn't stop bringing it up. I figured he had big plans for the money.

When I received the first $10,000 installment of my $40,000 inheritance from my mother, D hovered over my shoulder, staring at the amount. Cordial at that moment, he asked me what I would do with the money.

"Maybe I could get my teeth whitened?" I replied.

I had never really thought about my inheritance but when he asked me, a myriad of ideas popped in my head. I had no sooner offered up my secret wish when it became clear D already had other plans.

"You don't need your teeth whitened," he answered. "We're going to save this money and use it to put a new railing on the front porch," he said. "Besides, if you spend it right away, people will think you couldn't wait until your mother croaked."

All I could think about was my parents and I didn't care about the money. I did what was expected of me. I endorsed the check and deposited it in the bank.

After a few months, D began to talk about how much he could use a new pickup. He decided it was time to trade in his old one. Sure enough, he pulled into the driveway one day with a new silver pickup. With the trade in of his old one, he paid $10,000 cash.

16

Doctor Visit

AS THE SYMPTOMS ATTRIBUTED TO Fibromyalgia worsened, I continued to see doctors. I wondered if my mind was making my body sick. I hurt all over, and I continued to have balance problems. My hair was falling out because I had a chronic itching scalp that would often turn scabby. There was no obvious explanation, just the diagnosis of a vague disease that can have a variety of symptoms ranging from numbness in extremities to cognitive difficulty.

One day in early 2005, while beating the pavement of the mall to pick up something for D, I passed a hair salon. Because my hair looked terrible from the chronic skin problems, and with just enough saved money to afford it with a small tip, I made the impulsive decision to cut my hair off after wearing it long all my life. The stylist cut it shorter than I wanted, and I began to worry about what D would think. As I slinked home, glancing at myself all the way in the rearview mirror, I felt uglier with each mile and felt the hairdo made me look far older than my 50 years. I began to worry about how D would react.

Sure enough, D went ballistic. I don't know if he hated it because I looked ugly, because I didn't ask permission, or because my hair was no longer as easy to grab. He berated me for hours and then seemed pissed at me for days with lingering insults about which butch women I most resembled.

With my hair falling out and my symptoms from Fibromyalgia worsening, I went to see Dr. Helms for a checkup. Dr. Helms was a kind doctor that I had seen for years and had grown to trust. As I sat on the examining table feeling ugly and low, his questions picked open a wound that began bleeding the secrets of my miserable marriage. Whether I thought he might be the one to provide a remedy for it, or whether he just seemed like a safe sounding board to which I could purge my soul, I melted into a blubbering mess telling my secrets and crying as he handed me tissues. He looked shocked and tried to sooth me, but I could tell he didn't know what to do and finally suggested I contact the police. He had no idea that that was not an option because D had beaten me to the police with his Sunday afternoon bullshit sessions, and I didn't believe that the police would help me. I told him so.

He then questioned family support. I was too ashamed to tell him that I was estranged from my family. Defeated, he informed me that there was little he could do since he was tied to patient/doctor confidentiality. I wondered if he just didn't want to get involved. It was hard to imagine he couldn't help in any way, though most everyone, including myself, would surely do the same and turn a blind eye. Even though I got very little response from Dr. Helms, after sharing my secrets I felt lighter, but I had to face the reality of going back to my stale world.

Back I slogged. Upon returning home, I gave D as few details as possible about my doctor's visit, but he plied me for more. By this point in our marriage, I had come to realize that D could spin any tidbit of information against me. In perfect health his whole life, he couldn't relate to illness. D had no patience for my convalescence.

In fact, D was rarely even sick with a virus and in the 36 years I spent with him, I could probably count three times during that period that he had ever visited a doctor. According to D, he was the tough, rugged guy who didn't need to go to the doctor for every little thing, running up a doctor bill that was unnecessary. He expected me to buck up and do the same.

He was also too stubborn and tight to miss a day of work on the rare occasion he was sick. He was so possessive of the machinery he operated that he hated when another employee filled in to operate the same equipment. He believed no one was smart enough or man enough to run the crane. I often wondered about the validity of this but knew never to ask about it. Early in our marriage, D made it clear to me that I was to always stay out of his business and that I was not to be like "other fucking wives" that came down to the office and intercepted their husband's hard-earned paychecks.

One time, D had to stay home from work because he was miserable with a sinus infection. He made sure my day would be as fucked up as his. I couldn't cater to him fast enough, serving him meals, the mail, the newspaper, a pillow, a blanket and by late in the day he was subscribing to a beer cure, so I served them up too. I stayed out of the room when I wasn't required, as he groaned and complained from his recliner. Anything and everything made him mad. Even the news, local or national, riled him. He was worse than a sick baby who didn't get a nap. As I waited on him hand and foot, I both prayed he'd be well enough to go back to work the very next day, or that his ailment would kill him by sunrise.

Instead of donating to families that needed help to ease catastrophic illness, he'd condemn them for not having insurance in the first place and would say he'd be damned if he'd shell out money to help. If I tried to explain to D that many jobs didn't carry insurance on their employees and he was lucky that he worked for a company that did, he refused to listen. I had gotten so used to his cold-heartedness that rather than arguing and risk inspiring a tirade, I had taken to letting it go.

After my appointment with Dr. Helms and after my blood tests came back normal, I went to the Sunton drug store to fill the doctor's prescription for muscle relaxers to calm spasms associated with my Fibromyalgia. Although the drug helped the spasms, the side effects caused pounding headaches and lethargy. It numbed the nerves in my body and I could barely walk at times. I decided to stop taking the pills. When Dr. Helms wrote the prescription, I paid no attention to what he was prescribing, only to realize once I got home with it that it was the same drug that the Mayo Clinic had prescribed. With no intention of taking it with its nasty side effects, I stored it in the kitchen cupboard. I told D that I wouldn't take it anymore because it gave me headaches and made me dizzy.

About a month later, I noticed I was feeling tired and run down more than usual. All I wanted to do was sleep. I couldn't understand why, as blood tests a month earlier had revealed nothing. I chalked up my headaches to sinus infection, until one winter night in February, when D retrieved two bottled waters for us to drink as we watched TV. I found it odd that he would suddenly be thoughtful enough to offer me water. He never offered me anything. I thanked him but he said nothing.

By D's bedtime of seven, he got up and went to bed without saying a word, shutting the bedroom door to the living room. I reached for my water bottle and took a swig, thinking it tasted bitter. In a ray of light shining from the kitchen into the dark living room, I could see sediment floating in the remaining water in my bottle and a white substance collecting on the bottom. I usually refilled the plastic bottles with tap water to recycle them. I passed it off as lime forming on the bottom, as a result of reusing the bottles. I threw it in the garage and went to bed.

The next day as I opened the kitchen cupboard to retrieve a note pad, I noticed the muscle relaxer pill bottle was not exactly where I had left it. The thought dawned on me that D had tampered with my medication. I flushed the pills down the toilet and when I went to throw the pill bottle in the garbage, I noticed that the water bottle I had disposed of the night before, had a letter 'K' written on the bottom. With only two of us living in the house, there was only one of us who could have written it since it wasn't me.

Holidays

I N 2009 AFTER 40 YEARS with the company as equipment operator, D retired at the age of 58. I was relieved, even though it meant he'd be home more, because I mistakenly thought things would get much better between us without the stress and pressure from his job. It seemed that retirement suited D. I was looking forward to the future, especially holidays with family. But D was good at ruining family holidays and this resulted in our spending holidays alone. Thanksgiving Day arrived and D decided just the two of us would eat at a family restaurant 20 miles north of Sunton.

Ostensibly, we hadn't received invitations on either side of our families for Thanksgiving dinner. Much later, I would learn from my sisters, Evie and Ava, that they had indeed sent us an invitation, but D was the one who got the mail.

We had just pulled out of the driveway on our way to the restaurant when D started in on my family. After he insulted their eating habits, likening them to pigs, he belittled them for their poor manners in not inviting us.

"Well, no one in YOUR family invited us either," I said.

"Yeah, they did."

"Why didn't you tell me that?" I said.

"I did fuckin' tell you," D said, adding that he thought I was developing dementia like my mother and couldn't remember. D knew it would rile me up if he brought my mother into the conversation. Plus, it was a diversion tactic from the real conversation at hand, so I persisted, fueled with anger from the insult.

"Who from your side invited us?" I said. It was another question, and D hated questions.

"You know what your fuckin' problem is?"

I stared out the car window, waiting for the verbal assault to commence.

"You can't let me have one goddamn day without fucking it up," he shouted, smacking the steering wheel like he wished it was the top of my head. "If this is how it's going to be, I'm turning this mother-fuckin' car around and we're going home."

Knowing there was no way to diffuse the situation, the trapped side of me found an opening and I took it without forethought. "Go ahead and do it," I snapped. I was losing my fear of him. I no more got the words out of my mouth when he whipped a U-turn in the middle of the highway and began gunning it home where we didn't speak for the rest of the day and I ate left over soup. I'm not sure what he had, but I know his Thanksgiving celebration involved beer.

Christmas that year was another ruined holiday. We had been invited to a gathering of my family and I wanted to go, but it had snowed a bit and D used the dusting as the perfect excuse not to go. I told him I didn't think it was forecasted to accumulate.

"Go ahead and go to your fuckin' Christmas party, but I'm not going" he said. "See if I give a flying fuck if you get stuck in a snow bank. Don't bother to call me though, 'cause I ain't coming to dig your ass out."

I stood silent, knowing he meant every word as he started up again, using sarcasm.

"Oh, but that's right. You can't call me, 'cause you don't have a fuckin' cell phone," he said. "And you don't have a fuckin' cell phone, 'cause you ain't fuckin' important enough to have one."

I ignored him and got my prepared relish tray out of the refrigerator. D's temper continued to flare over my dismissal of the snow and he snatched the tray from my hands, socking me a blow with his hip as he slammed the enormous platter half on the counter, half into the sink.

"You ain't fuckin' going nowhere," he shouted.

As black olives rolled and bounced on the floor, I stood frozen wishing my family could see D's true colors instead of the nice guy he portrayed in front of them. Vegetables colored the kitchen counter and sink.

Keeping my head together, I took my first defensive step backward to put space between us. I was glad my hair was short. Menacingly, he pointed at the phone.

"Now, get on that fuckin' phone and call your goddamn brother and tell him we ain't coming."

My family was my weak spot. Though our relations were strained from the years of havoc D had wreaked, I clung to the TV-family hope that they would, in the end, rally behind me and show me a way out. He knew it was hitting below the belt. I knew that if we didn't show up to the party, my family would probably never speak to me again. And if I called and made a stupid excuse to cover for D's refusal to go, I would have to play like I was on D's side for he was sure to be listening in on my conversation. I was damned if I did and damned if I didn't. Either way, there was no escaping the wrath of D. Feeling like I was gutted, I chose not to call.

D ordered me to clean up the mess as he stomped from the kitchen and parked himself in front of the TV for the rest of the day. I gathered the vegetable remnants from the floor and dreamed of revenge. Mentally at war with D, I suppressed my hatred, hoping to give him a taste of his own medicine soon.

Car Ride

B

Y LATE SPRING OF 2010, we despised each other so badly that we barely spoke. D's need to bang me had even diminished. One Saturday morning he caught me off guard with a random offer of kindness, which he delivered with a twisted smile. He suggested we drive to Brownlo's Family Restaurant for Sunday brunch the next day. I was immediately suspicious of his motivation since it was so unusual for him to take me anywhere, but it was an outing and I couldn't resist. As contemptuous as I was of him, I was pathetic enough to cling to the dead fantasy that he might change and be nice to me—that I could have a respectable marriage and a decent life. As I chose to spin it positively, I became excited with the notion that we had a respectable date. I could hardly sleep that night.

We were scheduled to leave at 8:00 a.m. but by 7:45 a.m., D had already pulled the car out of the garage and was sitting there waiting for me with the car running. I scurried about trying to do some last-minute primping but I dared not keep D waiting and watch his mood plummet to the other pole. It was important to be early if the day was to start in peace.

We hadn't left the driveway when D criticized my weight. Enclosed in my own emotional armor, too elated by the prospect of fun, I didn't let the insult penetrate.

Since I ignored him, he next poked fun at my makeup calling me "clown face." I spun it as him paying attention to me.

The cool air warmed by the sun's rays brought a sparkling Sunday morning as the car ride filled with D's choice of '60s music blasting from the radio. The country pastures were peppered with cattle and farmers plowing. I saw spring; greened hillsides and ditches, and daffodil-graced gardens. The air streaming through our cracked windows was invigorating, minus an occasional wave of manure or skunk. Even that was part of the fun and made me belly giggle once.

Thirty minutes into our drive, I noticed what looked like a tunnel ahead created by overgrown trees that shaded the road. As we got closer, I began to feel anxious and claustrophobic about going through the tunnel. It felt like a warning. As we drove through the darkness of the tree tunnel, D suddenly added to my anxiety.

"You didn't tell anyone we were going to Brownlo's today, did you?"

I had to ask him to repeat himself.

"Did you tell anybody?" he said way too loudly.

"Tell anybody what?" I asked.

He grabbed my forearm and spewed, "That we're going to Brownlo's?"

"I told Ellie. Why?" I said, as I yanked my arm from him and the car swerved.

This appeared to be the wrong answer. His face reddened, and he squeezed his lips to contain himself. Finally, he burst as his palm pounded the steering wheel and "FUCK" roared from his mouth.

I couldn't understand the uproar. I'd been so excited about our outing, that I had shared it with a friend.

"You just ruined another fuckin' day for me," he cussed.

Keeping my emotions in check, I stared the floormat. I was afraid he would turn the car around in the middle of the highway and go home like he had that Thanksgiving Day, if I said anything, so I said nothing.

His rage had us speeding and we arrived earlier than anticipated as we pulled up to the front entrance of Brownlo's. He shoved the car into 'park,' jumped out and slammed his door, mumbling obscenities. I followed closely behind, trying to keep up with his bad mood.

A waitress brought water to the table and told us any time we were ready, to help ourselves to the buffet line. As she walked away, D snarled at her, blurting, "fuckin' bitch." At least it appeared he was referring to her and not me. It was loud enough for others to hear and I flushed with embarrassment. Though we rarely ate out, I was used to D treating the waitresses with disrespect. In his eyes, they were below him. I hated him for that, yet I didn't speak up either.

D got ahead of me as several people sandwiched between us, putting space between his growliness and my hunger pains. I forced a smile toward others as I stood in line, hiding my anxiety.

When D reached the front of the line, he slammed the serving utensils as he heaped huge helpings of breakfast sausages, bacon, and hash browns onto several plates along with a heaping plate of scrambled eggs. Hungry, I took a sample of everything, amazed at the assortment. I hadn't yet reached our table when I noticed D's plate half empty already. He refused eye contact as I arranged my plates on the table and sat down to eat.

Within minutes, D scarfed down the entire breakfast and asked the waitress for the bill. I rushed to finish my food, forfeiting the remainder of my plate because D was ready to leave within the space of twenty minutes.

With the peak of our excursion now behind us, I dreaded the ride home. I still wasn't sure why he was so angry but was certain I would find out sooner or later. As we walked through the restaurant to leave, I tried to hide behind D to avoid eye contact with anyone who had heard his foul mouth.

We had barely driven two miles before he ripped into me.

"Do you actually think you have friends left?" he said with an eerie calm that reminded me of the way Jack Nicholson talked to Wendy about midway through the movie, "The Shining."

"Because if you disappeared into thin air, nobody would give bull-fuckin' shit."

As he shoved death in my face, I found myself spiting the same for him. As the thought entertained my imagination, I reminded myself that I had no one in my corner, no resources, no recourse.

He didn't need an excuse to jump down my throat, he did it because it was his assumed entitlement as my husband. This time he directed his anger at my display of friendliness to others. My smile irked him. This was a pattern I had noticed in the past. It was as if he was jealous that I could still smile while his face wrinkled in anger. As D made choices to instigate drama, I made choices to keep a low profile with peace. Of course, the more I satisfied him, the better suited he was to tout dominance and control.

We drove home in silence from Brownlo's that day. Several times, I side-eyed D without turning my head only to see more contempt on his face. It was hard to notice the beautiful scenery or the smell of the earth because my mind now fixated on the cause of D's anger, as I replayed everything that lead up to his combustion. Why had my telling Ellie where we were going set him off? With too many murder mysteries playing in my head, I tried to block the worst-case scenario, but it darkened my thoughts and deepened my fears.

19

Rape

AFTER THE BROWNLO'S INCIDENT, I couldn't seem to shake the feeling that D wanted me gone from his life for good. I became suspicious of his every move, and especially leery when he poured on the charm. As if my marriage couldn't become any darker, D's contempt for me turned violent once again one night.

D was growing impatient with waiting for the largest installment of my inheritance money. Every day when the mail would come, he would beeline to the mailbox. One night, he brought up the subject up while we were getting ready for bed. He questioned me as to whether or not I had received checks without his knowing because he was convinced the money should have arrived by that point. I hadn't, of course, but he was working himself into a frenzy.

"You call your fuckin' sisters and find out what the damn problem is."

"No way. I'm not calling them because that makes me look greedy." It was an outright refusal, something I never did, and that was all it took. Immediately his adrenaline pumped full force, blackening his personality.

He lunged, shoving me backwards and slamming me to the bed. I knew what was coming. Anytime D's rage flared to this point, he would assert his dominance and show me who was boss. He yanked on the front of my jeans so hard the zipper broke. Reaching around me, he yanked my jeans over my butt, down to my feet, produced his rock-hard ego and began to shove it in and out as I lay limp. If I resisted, and he still won, it would empower him more, so I played dead. Besides, I was used to the routine of rough sex and knew it would be over soon. I usually watched the ceiling fan. I would try to follow a blade with my eyes. If the fan was on slow, I could do it but when it was on fast speed, it would beat me.

That incident of rape haunted me because it was different from most episodes. It was more violent and he had raped me with my clothes on, even tearing my clothes in the process.

One day, a week later and out of the blue, D asked if he had ever raped me. I was appalled but not surprised that he had the audacity to ask, and by asking, he further humiliated me and I lost control.

"You'll never stick that FUCKING DICK in me again," I shouted pointing at his crotch, releasing years of bottled rage. "From now on, I'm sleeping upstairs and I'm not coming down."

As D sat in the recliner taking it all in, his body slouched. It was the first time I had ever seen him speechless. I stomped off to our bedroom, gathering my pillow and other essentials and up the stairs I went to prepare my new bedroom. I never allowed him to violate me again.

Days later after he pulled himself together from my harsh penalty, he confronted me.

"I got to ask you something," he said.

Thinking it was serious, I stopped folding the laundry and gave him complete attention.

"So, when the hell did you dry up on me?" he asked, smirking his best smartass grin.

We stared at each other for what seemed like a minute and then I went back to folding clothes refusing to give him the satisfaction of a response. When he didn't get a rise from me, he chuckled.

"You know, you weren't nothing in bed anyway. Nothing but a dead log, a corpse. That's why I went elsewhere." The last few words slipped by his tongue before he realized what he had said.

Every cell in me wanted to cry but I'd be damned if I'd let him see me hurt. I turned away and left the room to return the laundry basket to the cellar. Minutes later, I could hear the porch door slam behind him.

I obsessed about his extra-marital confession, wondering how long it had been going on. I connected dots when I remembered seeing D's truck in the driveway of a woman who he knew. At the time I thought nothing about it because D had been helping her, supposedly cutting her grass when she had fallen on hard times. As I thought back on it, D had not been in her yard cutting her lawn when I had passed. A year later, while we were going through our divorce, I would find five tubes of K-Y™ Jelly in D's night stand.

As the months wore on, wretchedness wore a permanent frown on my face. Unaware of my scowl, one day a grocery store clerk asked how my day was going as I stood in the checkout line.

I replied, "Ok, I guess," as I stared the floor knowing my life sucked.

She smiled back and said, "Oh, it can't be that bad, can it?"

I turned my head away to fight tears. I thought about how I could so easily tell her, at that very moment, in front of other customers, the ridiculous story of my life. I was only three feet from her and felt so close to the solution to my dilemma, but it was like a death dream where you go to scream, and nothing will come out.

Abandoning family and friends to conceal secrets and continue the happy marriage charade, I was beginning to realize that I had lost myself as a person. Although D was to blame for the abuse in our marriage, I was to blame for the decision to marry him and the only one responsible for finding myself and fixing my mess.

20

The Beating

BY 2011 I BEGAN TO suspect that D was becoming more obsessed with my daily activities. He fixated on my timelines when I was permitted to take the car, always asking where I'd been and when I had gotten home for the day. More than once, I noticed him run his hand over the top of the car hood, upon returning home, checking for warmth, maybe dirt. On several occasions, I caught him checking the odometer, and inspecting tires. He seemed to be trying to catch me in a lie. I may have lied for him, but never to him.

After years of detailed inspections, it all came to a head one Saturday morning as D stomped into the kitchen from the garage, screaming obscenities.

"How in the hell did that front tire get all fucked up?" he yelled, his jowls hanging lower than ever.

Inching away from him and closer to the kitchen sink, I could smell something foul brewing. To stave off an all-out episode, I avoided his question. No matter what came out of my mouth at times like that, it was never going to be the right answer, so sometimes no answer worked best.

Since I hadn't given full attention to his absurd question, his anger unanswered, and since he hated silence, he found other sores to pick.

"Did you go to the bathroom in the middle of the night?" he asked.

"What difference does it make?" I said. "So, what?"

"There was toilet paper floating in the toilet this morning. You're wasting too much fuckin' toilet paper."

Right then, I made the mistake of turning the faucet on before I opened the cupboard and reached for a glass. I had done it in the wrong order.

"Turn that fuckin' water off. You're wasting so goddamn much water," snarled D.

I balked at his demand and as I mulled over the consequences, I continued to run the faucet.

D marched to the sink and slammed the faucet handle down, as I tried to step away. He caught me by the arm, thumb-printing my forearm blue, and swung me around to face his anger. I yanked my arm from him.

"Every weekend you waste water washing cars that aren't even dirty and how many times have you washed them when it's raining?" I blurted. "How much sense does that make?"

"Well, your lazy ass won't wash them. I'm the only one around here that does any fuckin' work." He puffed up to me with his chest rounding.

"If you want to lower the water bill, stop washing your cars," I said. It was a dangerous thing to say. No sooner had it soared past my lips with great bravado, I knew I had crossed the line.

"DON'T EVER FUCKIN' TELL ME WHAT TO DO," he shouted, grabbing the front of my shirt. I always knew the death grip was coming when his elbow went high. That provided a good angle to his hand so that when he grabbed the front of my shirt and twisted it clockwise, he would have enough torque to tighten my shirt into an instant harness. He pulled me toward his snapping face.

"As fuckin' crazy as you are, you need to get on some goddamn medication that keeps your fuckin' mouth shut," he bellowed, and then shoved me backwards, into the corner of the kitchen. The only place to go was down from there. I shielded my head with both arms as I cowered like a child. Because my hair was now short, instead of grabbing the back of my head, D grabbed the top, pulling me up, and I grabbed his hands to help lessen the force on my scalp. He slammed me against the refrigerator. It was always against the handles for maximum impact to my back and for the sake of rendering me stone-like. Next, he hit the side of my head, careful not to leave marks anywhere but beneath my hair, as his other hand dug into my jawline.

"You just can't keep your fuckin' trap shut, can you," he taunted, jamming his knee between my legs at my crotch, further pinning me to the refrigerator.

He continued to yank me around as if to get me lined me up just right. I kept trying to collapse to the floor with the fainting goat approach, but he kept heaving me upwards.

"You fuckin' cunt," he shouted.

He shook me violently and when he dropped me, I fell to the floor. I thought he was done, but he capped it off with a kick to my side and then another to my back. I lay on the floor groaning and crying.

"Get the fuck up," he yelled. As I tried to get to all fours again, he delivered a final kick to my tailbone and I fell forward.

In survival mode, I tried to obey, reaching for the handle on the kitchen cabinet, but the pain made me wonder if something was broken and I resorted to crawling away from him as he stood there with a smirk, arms folded, legs wide as if proud of his accomplishment.

I barely remember what followed and have only a vague memory of D leaving the house.

The kicks D delivered solidified his brutality. Later that day, I hobbled from the couch to the bathroom to assess the damage. As I stared in the full-length mirror, red and blue flesh spotted the bottom half of my body. It was my lower back that was most painful, making it excruciating to walk. It never occurred to me to take pictures of my bruises.

By the next day the pain was much worse, and I became bedridden. The couch became my home for the next two weeks while I recovered, giving me plenty of time to spend on refining my contempt for D.

In the first few days on the couch, my dreams were strange and my thoughts felt like kinked wire that you can't straighten. I began to wonder if other marriages were like ours and that maybe everybody covered it up like we did. We all just pretended in front of other people. Maybe it was common and was the perfect crime for men. In those first few days, this was a concept that helped me as I imagined I was part of a secret society of women and it felt good to belong to something.

D pretended nothing was wrong. He would come home from working at his part-time job as a groundskeeper for the City of Sunton, mentioning details of his day as if I was conversing with him, though I said nothing.

Over time, my thinking cleared with the bruises, but I had lingering pain trying to stand up or bend over. For the first time, I began to realize I was fitting the profile of a battered woman. My mindset was geared toward getting the son-of-a-bitch out of my life even if it killed me because if I stayed, *he* was going to kill me. I knew this, because I was getting less tolerant of him and the combustion that would result was destined to be dangerous.

Years later, an x-ray from a local chiropractor would reveal the source of the excruciating lower back pain I had suffered at D's heel and that continued to hurt. It was from a fractured tailbone.

21

Sam

AFTER MUCH TREPIDATION, I REALIZED the only way to be free was to rebel. But it was difficult to accept uncertainty. The patterns of behavior were well established. I knew it was a powder keg of a situation, yet I had to push back to progress toward freedom. The beating he had delivered left me wondering if I would be as lucky the next time he got his hands on me.

In the spring of 2011, D's short fuse lit again over the fact that the car was speckled with tar from road construction. I was to blame, since I last drove it.

As he slapped the back of my head, then tried to grab my hair, I elbowed my way out of his grasp, escaping behind the kitchen table to create a barrier between us. I grabbed the cordless phone along the way. D froze as we squared off, my finger prepared to dial. He stomped his foot to scare me into submission. I jumped and shrieked.

"I'm going to call the police or one of your brothers," I yelled. "Which one?"

"Which brother?" said D with a smirk, taunting me, assuming I would call neither. It wasn't easy for my shaking hand, but I dialed his brother Sam. D lunged and began to climb over the table, but Sam answered in the nick of time and D dropped back down to the floor.

"Sam, this is Kate," I said. "Sam, I need you to come over. Now. It's an emergency." D's face went scarlet. Sam wanted to know if anyone was hurt.

"Not yet," I said. "Just hurry."

Throughout our 25-year marriage, I had never involved his family or mine in our affairs. But desperate times called for desperate measures. Although I trusted no one, especially D's family, I figured that to expose D might curtail his actions. I knew it would do no good to call the Sunton Police.

As soon as I hung up the phone, D closed in on me, threatening to kill me if I told Sam what went on in our house. Our back and forth arguing, table between us, strengthened me to turn the tables and threaten him. The stronger I felt, the more arrogant I grew. I even donned an evil grin, to articulate my mood. D backed off.

"You just wait 'til Sam gets here and I tell him everything," I said, but it was more of a growl.

While D continued calling me every obscenity, he knew he needed to prepare himself to play the victim. He started by calming himself to appear the rational one.

The diesel truck pulled up and D ran outside to intercept Sam.

Ten minutes passed before Sam entered the kitchen without D, dead-staring me as if I was the instigator and the bully to his blameless brother.

Hyped with adrenalin, I paced the floor, puffing on yet another cigarette. From the few words Sam and I exchanged, it was obvious whatever I said would not trump his loyalty to D.

I yelled at Sam, telling him that D warned me to keep my big mouth shut or I'd be "one dead fuckin' bitch." Sam downplayed D's quick temper as nothing more than me pushing D's buttons, advising me to back off and stop getting him more riled up than he already was. This further angered me, but I understood that blood was thick, and forced myself to calm down. I was afraid to tell Sam that D had taken to beating me, so I hinted at it, telling him that I had been unable to get off the couch for two weeks after my last argument with D.

After I had revealed much ugliness and shed many tears, Sam left. D intercepted him outside the porch door. I knew he would. D needed to know what I had said in order to twist my words. D had to be in control of the information. To remain top dog, he had gotten to Sam first, and would get to him last.

Seconds after Sam's truck pulled away, D stomped into the house, swearing well before he reached the kitchen. He demanded to know what I had told his brother. I didn't know if Sam had refused to share the information, or if D wanted to check my account against Sam's. Sarcasm rolled from my tongue as I puffed my chest bigger than D's.

"When you stop lying about me, I'll stop telling the truth about you," I said in an evil whisper.

The smell of revenge angered D and his nostrils flared like bellows. I felt invincible at that moment as we stared down truth in the air between us.

From that point forward, the war was in full swing as D's patterns of hidden agendas became more complicated and secretive. While he continued playing mind games with me, I continued paging through the instruction manual in my brain on how to beat him at his own game.

22

Reappraisal

THE MORE I LEARNED THAT D had name-dropped 'crazy bitch' to others, the more the dark corner of my imagination blackened. As I wore down, my bitterness grew and developed scenarios of suffering that could befall D. I was particularly fond of imagining a slow suffering disease that would permanently debilitate him. I didn't want him dead. I wanted him to suffer. It needed to match the same slow hell he had put me through. I was living what I had learned, playing the same revenge game D played on me. His deceit was contagious.

All my stifled rage had turned me into a bitter person. With the lava of secrets flowing underneath the hatred, my anger was erupting in small ways. Not to D, but to unsuspecting and undeserving folk in stores, the post office, or gas station. I was impatient in lines and would complain loudly to others. I would scream with road rage in the car where no one could hear me. It wasn't me and the conflict between the grief and my nature made me feel like I really was losing my mind. I would scold myself with the reminder that I had to stay sane, or at least appear sane, just to survive.

The reality was that I was doomed in every way because D was the wizard behind the curtain. Whereas I had felt so worthless after losing job after job, now I had come to believe that D was even behind my terminations. I was destined to fail. My failure fit his game because it provided material for him to belittle me. He portrayed me as worthless to my face, and mentally incompetent to others while he bragged that he himself was the sole 'breadwinner' of the family. With every job termination, D sucked me down into depression, faulting me that I couldn't keep my big mouth shut. Of course, when problems arose at my job, D would lure information from me and would dictate my actions accordingly. Like an automaton, I had done exactly what D had told me to do never realizing what a puppet I had become. At my last job I had come across as too aggressive, opinionated, or contrary, and that played into my termination. It wasn't me talking, it was D talking through me. Once unemployed, I completely relied on D and he used it to great effect, controlling me with money. Without work, I was confined to the house. Isolation kept me lonely and fear kept me his. Packaged as a mentally ill person, I imagine now that I appeared to others too paranoid to come out of hiding and show my face.

The caution flags waved strong, yet I had not read into it as it was happening. I didn't realize how bad it had gotten until I stepped back and assessed the damage. Slowly, year after year, having adapted to D's nastiness that grew to brutality and abuse, I learned to adjust to his thug mentality because thinking for myself came with consequences. By the time it got so bad, I was in too deep to dig myself out, seemingly stuck with him forever.

The illusion that D set forth of me for nearly 40 years had a lasting effect on everyone. Years later, I would learn the destruction to my relationships would be irreversible and I would never be able to right it. D had everyone snowed. During those days, nobody stepped forward to expose D's dastardly deeds. They didn't know it was dastardly. They thought it the truth. That day of reckoning would happen years later.

I had come to realize that the longer I stayed, the more difficult it was to leave. I knew I needed to go. It was past time. I needed to build myself up first and be optimistic in order to see the possibilities of a brighter future. If I wanted it badly enough, I would have to be brave. I would have to be willing to suffer other fears.

23

Sisters

ONE MORNING, LESS THAN A week after I called Sam to expose D's abuse, D continued to grill me, wanting to know what I had leaked to Sam. I refused to answer him. When he realized that I wasn't going to tell him what I discussed with Sam, he tried another tactic.

D suggested I move back downstairs to our bedroom as the heat upstairs wasn't good for my Fibromyalgia. I scoffed at his veiled excuse. D had never once driven me to a doctor's appointment at the Mayo Clinic or Iowa City. He did not accompany me for either of my carpal tunnel surgeries, and of course, he dropped me off at the door for the surgery that erased the possibility of children from my life. But now, D was concerned about my health.

Figuring that an appeal to my Fibromyalgia issue would make me putty, D was sure just like all the other times, he'd entice me back into his good graces, that I would spill the information he so badly wanted, and I would go back to servicing him in his bed. The heat and humidity in the upstairs bedroom would stand strong as my preferred sleeping environment. I ignored D, standing with my arms crossed as if I was in total control, yet knowing at any minute he could turn on me and slam me to the wall.

When I refused to speak to him, he changed course again.

"So, what time did you leave the graduation party?" he asked, referring to my god child's celebration that he had refused to attend. At first, I wasn't sure where he was going with it and then I realized that he might be testing my answer against his friend Barney's. Barney had been at the party and I had a sneaking suspicion that he had been watching me.

Barney was an old friend of D's from the early '70s. Upon D's convincing, he moved to Iowa from Colorado after retirement. I can only imagine what D had promised him to relocate to Sunton. He was nothing more than a brain-fried hippy from the dope he smoked, the speed he took, and the acid he dropped. He would brag about it as someone would brag about their professional accomplishments. His bald head was crowned with thinning strands of long gray hair pulled back into a ponytail. His immature demeanor was not unlike the elementary kids he taught in Colorado. Gullible and naïve, Barney was an easy target for D's manipulation.

I stayed silent for several minutes before responding to D's 'time' question.

"What difference does it make?" I asked.

He ignored me, repeating the question with hands stapled to his hips.

"So, what time was it?" he demanded.

Cynicism spit from my lips from the fury of that graduation day when D refused to go.

"Well, if you'd gone with me to Terry's graduation party in the first place, you'd know exactly what time I left the party. But, oh no," I said. "You just had to find an excuse to stay home."

"It wasn't my goddamn fault. There was fuckin' work to be done and I can't party every damn time you want to," he said.

I was sick of the lame excuses. My family was my weak spot, estranged or not, and my temper flared.

"You have an excuse every damn time," I said. "Those new garage doors laid in their boxes for months. Funny how you just had to install them the Sunday of the graduation party."

As he stood at one end of the kitchen table waiting for the answer he wanted, I kept a safe distance on the opposite end of the table.

Roaring, he lashed out, "I asked you what fuckin' time you left that damn party."

"Oh you mean Barney didn't tell you," I mocked, "You sent him to spy on me."

If the last five years of living with D taught me anything, it taught me I was in for one physical battle of my life as D was clearly struggling to accept that I was taking control of myself and didn't need him anymore.

Silence hung in the air and then he belted in anger.

"You didn't answer my fuckin' question," he shouted.

I gritted my teeth for I'd be damned if I'd give up anything this time.

Then the phone rang. D's demeanor instantly camouflaged his toxic side when he answered the phone.

"Oh, yeah Evie, she's right here."

Still feigning pleasantries, he handed me the phone.

"Kate. It's your sister, Evie," he said, glaring at me.

Unable to switch emotional gears myself, I was short and rude to Evie at first as I listened to the obligatory small talk about her teaching schedule. Then the conversation took a turn.

"Listen," said Evie, "Ava and I were thinking about driving up to Sunton to take you out to lunch, like a girl's day out. The three of us have never done that."

I was so taken aback by her invitation that I almost laughed out loud. This was very out of character for my sister. It was quite obvious she was up to something.

I was still simmering in attack mode and I couldn't let my guard down with D standing before me. Yet here was a chance to reconnect with my family, something I considered extremely important. I stumbled on my words and didn't know how to answer. This was something that the old Kate would have to say "no" to and provide a valid lie as to why I wouldn't be available. Times had changed. Evie persisted, reminding me we were getting older and it would be nice to stay connected. Stifling my fear of D, I accepted the invitation.

"I'd love to," I said. "When would you guys like to get together?"

Evie seemed floored that I actually agreed for once. We made plans to see each other in two weeks. I circled the date on the large office calendar sprawled over the counter top, as D hovered over my shoulder.

I barely hung up the phone before D cut loose.

"What the fuck was that all about?"

Knowing I had the upper hand, I was going to enjoy letting him know I wasn't asking permission.

"Evie and Ava are coming up to take me out to lunch," I said, an air of pride exuding from me.

"Well, I ain't going to be here," he pouted.

'I wouldn't want you to be here," I answered back. "It's for us three sisters only, a girl's day out."

I could see the muscles in D's jaw flexing and relaxing, flexing and relaxing. People were getting too close to me and he realized his control was melting. The gears were turning in his head over how to best proceed and submission was becoming a good route for D. It was a route he resented, but D was not stupid, as he felt the control shifting with the knowledge that I had the goods on him and would share. The day ended without serious drama and I continued to sleep upstairs in the heat. When I would get sweaty, I took to pretending I was on a deserted beach, baking in the sun.

Several weeks later, the day of the sister-reunion arrived. I was eager yet nervous about their visit as I had only seen them from a distance at Terry's graduation. None of us had sought one another out. Now they were coming to see me and I didn't know why. Would I pretend everything in my life was normal and I was content? Would I spill the beans and tell the truth? Part of the truth? Just the basics? All of it would be too much. Could I just tell them that my marriage was so bad that I had moved upstairs? What if they asked why?

As I fidgeted at the window, I tried to remember the last time they were at my house for a visit. It had been 10 or 15 years. I remembered the night Evie and her husband had dropped in on the way back from their son's basketball game against Sunton. Around 10 p.m., I woke D up. He had fallen asleep early, sloshed with alcohol, and was livid. For the days that followed, D had hounded me about never waking him up again just to bullshit with my family.

I continued pacing the floor as I took a drag from a cigarette. I tried to keep an open mind as to my sisters' mission. Something was up.

When Evie's white car pulled into the driveway, I plastered a grin on my face as I greeted them at the back door. They did the same, but we didn't hug for we weren't that close anymore. As we passed through the living room to get to the kitchen, I sidestepped, and noticed their eyes circling the room. There were no Klaver family pictures, only pictures of D's family and walls filled with D's toys. I never noticed it until then, how much the house was filled with only D's things. Two hallways, the living room, dining room, parlor, and the two upstairs bedrooms were filled with D's expensive toys displayed to museum quality perfection. You couldn't tell I lived there.

Evie, Ava and I settled into the kitchen with an air of uneasiness. I lit another cigarette while they seated themselves at opposite ends of the table. They glanced around the room, saying nothing. I prided myself on an immaculate kitchen and house. Having children and grandchildren themselves, I'm sure my house appeared sterile. It was close to 11:30 p.m. and I was starved, hoping we'd leave immediately to find a local restaurant. However, the awkwardness continued as I glanced at Evie and Ava who were feigning smiles. I noticed a resemblance in our aging jaws and hereditary moles I had never noticed before.

Ava began tapping fingers on the table as I stood behind her. It's always been a nervous habit she didn't know she had. It put me on edge, but I didn't say anything because I didn't want to start a tiff.

Attempting to strike up a conversation, Ava stopped tapping her fingers and wrung her hands.

"So," Ava said. "What's D up to today?"

"I don't know. He didn't want to be here when you guys came," I said, testing honesty at the start.

Evie stared at Ava and then eyed my discomfort. Ava continued.

"Oh. How come he didn't want to see us?" she said.

The inquiry from my sister touched a raw nerve. I wanted to tell everything. I had wanted to tell them for so long and as the opportunity presented itself, and since they were asking, it began to boil. Before I knew it, I was telling the whole story.

So much poured from me that my sisters had difficulty processing what I was trying to tell them. Stories began to bottleneck. It was my recounting of the tubal ligation that did them in. They were not only mothers, they were Catholic. Motherhood was the largest part of their lives and identities. To deny a woman motherhood was repulsive to them. Upon hearing for the first time the real reason D and I had never had children was more than they could bear. They were speechless.

Evie's hands gripped her temples, shocked by my confession and the emotional dehydration of my life. Panicked, Ava rose from the table and paced the floor.

"Kate, you've got to get your typewriter out and write a book," she said, desperate to offer a solution, however clumsy.

They knew I was telling them the truth. I had no reason to lie and hide secrets unless forced. As teachers, they were well aware of the ripple effects domestic violence plays on a student's frame of mind. Though they were trained to recognize symptoms of abuse, it was inconceivable that their own sister could be a victim. D had thrown them off the scent all those years with stories of my mental instability. Sifting through layers of lies unraveled a narcissistic, pathological liar of a brother-in-law, and Evie and Ava had trouble processing the information.

A heavy burden lifted from my shoulders that day as decades of secrets flowed. A powerful shift took place in me as I realized I was still in denial about my marriage. I had been living a lie and not a life and it was time to admit it to all. Exposing the truth of my tormented marriage to my sisters became the tool I needed to push forward for change.

I would learn that what prompted their visit were rumors that had spread to the elementary school where they both taught. Hearing that D was getting closer to committing me, Evie and Ava decided to see for themselves what they could do to find help for my so-called mental illness. Informing them that I was not the crazy one threw them into a tailspin. Trusting D all those years, they had come to believe that he had provided a stable and comfortable home for me, unknowing that under our roof, D was the devil himself.

24

Help Arrives

AFTER THE LUNCH WITH MY sisters, and the yoke of secrets had been lifted from my neck, I felt much better knowing my family finally understood the circumstances that had isolated me from them all those years.

Then, nothing happened. There was no outcry. There was no family showing up with a moving truck to secure my release. There were no phone calls. No one checked on me.

I realized I had not exactly offered up a plan or even the slightest request for help, but I assumed they would take over like revolutionaries in a coup. They might show up under the cover of darkness, barricade D in his bedroom and spring me with all my belongings. We'd high five in the end and I would tell them they were my heroes.

Whittling away the safe feeling I had had after my sisterhood confession, weeks passed as my hopes were dashed that the cavalry would arrive. I began to revert to the old mindset that I was trapped, that my family didn't care. D and I were still playing a mind-control dance and staying out of each other's way as much as possible. We barely spoke. My spirits continued to tank and my nerves were shot. Neck and shoulder spasms plagued me and grew worse by the day.

D knew something was up since my lunch with Evie and Ava. His deceitfulness worked well as long as we did not compare notes. I could feel him sensing the ripple in his plan. There was a creepy calm about him. He moved more quietly around me and eyed me more from the side when he thought I wasn't looking. I thought he might be done physically beating me because with the glowing light from the end of the tunnel, he knew he could not get away with abuse anymore. That didn't mean a wrecking ball couldn't fall on my head.

Then, one mid-morning about a month after the fateful lunch with my sisters, a white truck pulled into the driveway. I cracked the back door open to see who the driver might be. Out jumped a man I didn't recognize at first because the bill of his cap was pulled down obscuring his face. As he walked closer to the back steps, I realized it was my brother, Doug. I couldn't believe it. Then, I doubted his intentions. Maybe he had just stopped because he was working in the area.

I ran down the steps with hope and tears and sure enough, my brother wrapped his big bear arms around me in the biggest hug I had had in a quarter century or more. He lifted me off my feet.

"You okay?" he asked.

"Yeah," I said, realizing how unconvincing I was since I was crying. "But you can't stay because if D comes home and sees you, I'll have hell to pay later."

"Get all your stuff, 'cause we ain't coming back," said Doug, with a look that rivaled Rambo.

"Doug, I can't. It's bad timing," I said, my brain somersaulting. "I have too much stuff to figure out. I can't just leave. Maybe if you had given me a little more notice." I was feeling an all-out anxiety attack about to fall upon me, racing heart and all.

"Is he really beating you?" said Doug.

"He roughs me up alright," I said. "It's not real regular, but I don't trust him at all. He's got a bad temper, Doug. He's a mean son-of-a-bitch."

"Well, the family has never seen any marks or bruises on you, Kate," Doug said, testing me.

"Oh hell no. When D slams be into walls and the refrigerator, you can't see bruises on my back and legs," I hiccuped and thought I might puke as I kept an eye on the road for D's truck.

"Come on Kate, we've got to get out of here before D gets back," persisted Doug.

"Doug, you gotta go without me this time and I promise I'll get ready to go and let you know when is good."

"Well, if you won't go let's do this," said Doug, pulling a business card out of his pocket. "Let's put the fear of God in him by letting him know I was here. You throw this on the counter and he'll know."

When Doug drove away that day, I was more fearful than ever with the walls closing in on D. What would be his next move? How would it end?

Minutes later, D jerked his truck into the driveway and stomped into the house. I said nothing and as soon as his eyes had scanned every surface for irregularities and had intercepted Doug's business card, I had the satisfaction of seeing it register in his brain. I turned to retreat to my upstairs bedroom where I barricaded the door. That night I didn't sleep, terrified he'd get a piece of me and never let go until I no longer existed.

Days later, D would leave a message on Doug's answering machine, saying he felt it was in my best interest that the Klaver family get me on medication as I was supposedly out of control, destroying the house. It was D's last-ditch effort to ruin me. But now, my family knew better.

I would learn much later that soon after their lunch with me, Evie and Ava had called a family meeting to inform everyone about my situation and the severity of it. From that meeting, they rallied to get me out without calling the police, and my brother Doug was nominated to perform the rescue.

25

Divorce

IT WAS D WHO FINALLY brought up the word divorce, early in the summer of 2011. I was floored at first, but whereas I was unable to imagine the possibility before, once he opened the door, Catholic tradition be damned. My imagination unleashed. D had tossed the word around casually many times in the past, like when I had had my tubes tied, but it was a control technique then, not a serious threat. In fact, D always couched it in an ultimatum to me, over which I had the control to choose to obey him or be the scourge of society. I would have been the bad guy had I chosen the latter. Now that things had fallen apart so badly, the word divorce rang louder than wedding bells. There was no containing the momentum or pining away for some stupid antiquated custom of staying married at all costs. Once the notion was in my head, I couldn't believe how foolish I had been.

This time, I would find out if he was bluffing again. I took the bait.

"No love loss there. We should never have gotten married," I said, affirming the idea of divorce.

To drive the point home, I lied to him for the first time and told him that I had an attorney already.

"You don't have any money to hire a fuckin' attorney," he said.

I mirrored the same devilish smirk D had always sneered at me, the one I had practiced for years. He clammed up. Though I was bluffing, it was a cheap thrill to watch him squirm.

Feeling me slipping away, D tried coaxing his right hand to my waist in an effort to stem the marital bleeding. I pulled away from his grasp as he told me it wasn't too late to reverse things and start over.

D's arms reached out again, attempting to hug me but I shooed him away and stepped further from him. I began detailing the myriad ways he controlled me and how I couldn't take it anymore. He became defensive, trying to convince me that I got everything wrong. I went on to tell him that I had discovered what he'd been doing behind my back, tainting my reputation as crazy.

D tried to play his final card, a clumsy attempt to smooth the 36 years of hell. He suggested I go see his mother as if she would suddenly sprout a heart for me and confide in me the knowledge of how to be happy with her son. I wrinkled my nose and dropped my jaw. The thought made me incredulous.

"You want me to talk to your mother?" I smirked. "You're a 60-year-old man and you're still crying to your mother?" Instead of flying into a murderous rage over the slight, D knew I was slipping from his control and he became someone else, reaching in the dark.

"Yeah. I know mom will set things straight."

"Your mom hasn't exactly been nice to me because you turned her and your entire family against me," I said, shouting. "So I doubt she'd give a damn about me now."

"You're just jealous that I GOT a mom and yours is fuckin' dead," D fired back, with wolves closing in on him. His nasty words that once bit hard didn't faze me now. I was aware he was changing the subject to deflect blame as usual. The old D again.

"Unlike you, I never once ran to mommy and daddy, complaining about the hell you put me through," I cried.

Confronting D head on with the reality of my feelings stunned him. I was sure he believed he'd never get caught in his own lies. His arched back now hunched as he aged ten years in that moment being whacked with the truth that I owned.

"You'd be surprised what people have been telling me of what you've been doing behind my back," I said. "I've been watching you real close as to where you go."

"Well, I don't know who the fuck you've been talking to, but they're fucked up in the head to even be talking to a crazy bitch like you," he said.

"I've always had your back, bragging about you and never once did I tell anyone how cruel and abusive you were to me, thinking you'd change, but you never did. You only got meaner." My voice was still rising.

"You know what your fuckin' problem is?" asked D.

"Yeah. IT'S YOU," I bellowed. "Why would you be so spiteful and mean to me all those years for no reason why?"

D spit frothy saliva and his body seemed to quake.

"Because I can. Because I fuckin' can and everyone believes me," he said, admitting to the pathology of his ways for the first time. "Besides, who's going to believe a crazy cunt like you over me?"

He had a valid point. I was worried about who would believe me, but I realized if I pushed D into a corner and told the truth to all, he'd weaken and falter. D's need to be well respected in the community was crumbling and paranoia was pushing him over the edge of sanity as we both struggled to attain rights to me.

As I worked to find an attorney for real, D beat me to the punch. I received papers in the mail. Knowing now that I had too much on him, he wanted me out of his life more than ever. Ordering me to move out, he bragged the house would be all his in the divorce, so I might as well get used to living somewhere else. I told him I wasn't budging from my comfy upstairs bedroom. When that didn't work for him, with two fingers in my face—knowing he couldn't touch a hair on my head because I would definitely call 911—D threatened to commit me to a psych ward.

"Two fuckin' signatures and I'll put you away forever 'cause ain't nobody going to believe a cunt like you. Everybody already knows you're fuckin' crazy cause I made sure of that."

"Ahh, but you're wrong there because you see," I taunted back with attitude, "my whole family knows about you. Sam knows. I told my attorney. My doctor knows everything. The neighbors know. People are on to you, D," I sniped. "You've been talking and so have I."

As I backed away from him, D nudged closer, prodding for answers.

"Just what the fuck did you tell everybody?" he rasped through gritted teeth, lips curled tight against them.

"I'll answer that when you admit all the lies you've been spreading about me," I said.

Of course, D would do no such thing as he stomped from the house. I smiled at how good it felt to shut him up for once, but his threat about two signatures began to haunt me. I knew it was possible for him and another to commit me, because I had done the same to my father years earlier. I began to obsess about it and could feel the fear my father must have felt when he was told he would be locked away.

26

Attic Door

WITH DIVORCE LOOMING, D MADE my life more difficult than ever. He wanted me to move out of the house. If he could get me to leave, he could tell the world he was abandoned by me, his perfect crime sealed. Intimidation was his best game to prompt me. I was determined to tough it out and refused to be the one to leave. I was less scared of him, feeling safety in the numbers of people who knew the truth. If I ended up dead, D knew all fingers would point at him.

D entered my upstairs bedroom often, rummaging through things when I wasn't home, looking for anything to use against me. I doubt he found much as I kept all documentation secured in the car trunk with both sets of keys tucked in my purse, which I stowed away in rotating hiding places. When D couldn't find evidence of my future intentions, he shifted gears, setting folded bath towels at the edge of my bed trying the 'nice guy' approach. Although my nerves were stretched thin, I wasn't about to cave. Instead, I told him if he ever stepped foot in my bedroom again, I'd call the cops.

I got into the habit of duct taping my bedroom door shut. I would mark it here and there with tiny 'x's so I would know if the tape had been repositioned.

One hot humid Saturday morning while I sat in the recliner watching TV, D tried yet another approach to get me to come back downstairs and sleep with him. Working himself into a frenzy, he hauled wood and tools up the stairsteps in the back, hammering and drilling and making all sorts of noise. I wondered what the commotion was all about but refused to take to the stairs because I was certain D was expecting my nosiness. Refusing to give him the satisfaction, I waited it out, all the while nervous as to what he was doing to my bedroom door. Used to his best days being my worst, I had made up my mind, whatever he had done, I'd deal with it somehow.

Two hours later, he hopped in his truck and pulled out of the driveway. I knew he was headed toward Barney's for his usual Saturday afternoon drunkenness.

As soon as I couldn't hear D's truck anymore, I ran up the stairs to see what he had done. Nothing seemed out of place, but I noticed how much hotter it was. When I looked toward the end of the hallway toward the door that entered the attic, I saw that D had replaced the attic door with a homemade screen door. The heat poured through the screen.

D thought he would cook me out and that that would be a logical solution to ending the stalemate.

I went to work duct taping doubled-up bedsheets to the screen door to keep the heat from flowing through the screen. Feeling proud of myself for conquering his dirty deed, I sat down to resume watching Saturday afternoon TV.

Hours later, I heard D's truck arrive. He came through the door wasted, and high-stepping. He looked so drunk. I was impressed that he had found his way into the house. He made his way up the stairs to check his attic screen, bracing himself between both sides of the wall in the narrow staircase. I could hear him swearing and cussing, then, the sound of duct tape ripping. When he made it back down the stairs, he was holding the huge wad of doubled sheets striped with duct tape. He staggered to my chair, blocking me into it as I braced myself for an explosion.

Throwing the wadded sheets in my face, he yelled, "What the fuck is this shit?"

I grabbed the ball of sheets and aimed directly at his face with the exact response. "Yeah, what the fuck IS this shit?"

He flipped switches. "Well, I was trying to do something nice for you by letting all the hot air out of the attic so it would cool down the house." He got closer to my face as if trying to flirt. His breath repulsed me.

"You let all the hot air IN and not OUT and you know it," I said with a look that told him not to fuck with me. I even leaned into it.

D stood swaying back and forth as his head bobbed like a dashboard dog. He was too drunk to argue with me and turned away to stumble to his bedroom.

I puffed hard on my cigarette, proud that I held strong and dished it back. In that moment, I even realized I liked myself when I was detached from D.

While D passed out in the bedroom, I made attempts to cover the attic entrance once again with sheets and more duct tape. The ceiling fan in my bedroom was worthless that night as I roasted anyway. Unable to stand it any longer, I found a razor blade and managed to cut the dried paint around the window sill. It took an eternity, bruised fingers, and buckets of sweat, but I managed to pry the damn thing open, releasing the hot stuffy air from the room.

27

Safeguards

PLAYING THE GAME OF LIFE, I had to be wiser in order to win. Little by little, I was gaining ground while he was losing it. He was scrambling to save himself while continuing to portray me as crazy, but I refused to give up or give into his demands. Not only was I refusing to ever go back to his bed, despite the heat wave in my bedroom, I refused to give him the TV remote when he demanded it. The remote became an important item. Whereas before I had always relinquished the remote when D requested it, now, since I had called Sam, the remote was as much mine. The little plastic device no longer had just the power to turn on the TV; it had the power to overthrow our domestic government. D wanted the remote and I wanted control. I slept with it under my pillow to ensure its safety.

I refused to budge and he refused to stop threatening committal. To prove I had even more control, I blasted the TV so he couldn't sleep while I stayed up late. It was childish, but it was all I had, and hatred and a marriage undone does funny things. He'd scream at me to turn the TV down, threatening to cut the cable if I didn't. I knew D was bluffing because he was too obsessed with the Discovery and History channels to be without cable TV. I can only assume D continued to lose sleep as I played the TV loudly into the wee hours of the morning.

One August afternoon, I was getting ready to go to see an old girlfriend, Jenna, who I had recently happened upon in the grocery store. Jenna and I had known each other since high school. We had lost touch at times because of her husband's work transfer, but since reconnecting, we slipped easily back to our high school bond and she became my confidant. Jenna and her husband had invited me to their home for dinner as I had told her I was going through a nasty divorce.

Upon noticing I was getting dressed up to meet Jenna, D started in. With his paranoia in full swing, he demanded again that both sets of car keys be handed over. I knew he was trying to stop me from having any form of communication with others but I refused to relinquish the keys. I mouthed back that the car was mine and that he had the truck and two muscle cars to take him where he needed to go. That was all it took.

He went to grab my shirt but I was quick and escaped.

"If you don't give me those goddamn keys and now, I'm going to throw all your fuckin' clothes out on the front lawn."

"Go right ahead because if you do, it will be my turn to throw your valuable toy tractors one by one, box and all, on the lawn" as I flipped him the bird and said, "Fuck you."

"You're bluffing," he said with a stare that looked like it could pierce skin.

"Try me," I smarted back.

D wasn't going to take a chance on having his toys trashed, for those were his most valuable treasures. He backed off and stomped away, his body ready to combust.

I won that round as I continued getting ready to see Jenna. It was a relief to have her support and the support of her husband, Jay. Jenna would be the one to convince me to get a post office address, a checking account, and a cell phone in going forward with the divorce.

I had dinner at Jenna's that night and when I got home, D had removed piles of his clothes and was chucking them into the front seat of his truck. I assumed he was going to stay at Barney's. It shocked me that he didn't have the will to tough it out but he knew his temper. Later, in a police report, D told the responding officer that he was afraid to stay at the house any longer because he was afraid that I was trying to provoke him.

In the month he stayed with Barney, he came home every day, spying on me, riffling through my bedroom, checking mail, snooping phone messages and redials, finding every excuse to continue stalking me. I was careful to keep all paperwork locked in the car trunk. My purse became so overloaded that I had to resort to a larger tote to accommodate everything.

At night, to be safe, I would place a chair underneath the door knob believing D, with the help of his brother Sam, would take me against my will and commit me in the wee hours of the morning like we had done to my dad. Paranoia dogged me. D's brother Sam had been around way more than usual and I thought they were in cahoots about something.

Plus, I had heard a story, years earlier, about a woman from Sunton whose husband got her committed. He was a mean guy and I could only imagine how awful he was as a husband. In a small town where bar room gossip spreads fast, I had heard that her husband had locked her out of the house in the dead of winter one morning after she stepped outside to get the paper. Unable to get in the house, she was forced to run across the highway to the neighbor's house to avoid freezing. It all made her look crazy and she ended up in MHI—the Mental Health Institute in Pensha. Whether the story was true or not, I'm not sure, but I knew he was mean enough to do it and now the story haunted me with new vengeance. D also knew the story well.

The silence between us was growing louder by the day. Believing D was up to something, in order to calm my fears, I decided it would be beneficial for me to contact the neighbors next door and make them aware of my drama and any potential violence that might result.

One early evening, when D wasn't home, I slipped over to the neighboring couple's house and told them everything. I purged my grief and the more I talked, the madder I got, and the madder I got, the more I smoked until I had smoked my entire pack of cigarettes and was sponging cigarettes from them.

The next day, my lungs burned raw and my head exploded a horrific sinus headache. I didn't plan to quit smoking, it just happened. Cold turkey. It was the beginning of never having my clothes stink from cigarette smoke again. Besides, I couldn't afford the daily $5.00 price tag a pack of cigarettes brought at that time.

Less than a month later, D moved back. Once again, he tried to make himself the victim by removing the garage TV, hauling it down the cellar steps, setting it up on a large wooden shelf, and connecting wires and cables for fine tuning. Next, he hauled a reclining lawn chair down the cellar steps, accessorizing it with a pillow, and his blanket. He displayed several magazines for an added touch of hominess. It was all a setup to invoke empathy from others.

When his family and friends would stop by, he would invite them to the cellar, showing them all where he slept and watched TV, complaining I wouldn't allow him access to the upstairs. He appeared the martyr who had been banished to the dungeon.

Jenna, who had helped me get a cell phone, now decided I needed a new email address since D and I shared the old one. This way, I didn't have to worry when I corresponded back and forth with my attorney. I hid my flip-phone in my bra cup because I didn't want D to know I owned one and I didn't trust him to not rummage through my purse, so I hid my purse too. D's unpredictability had me spinning in circles, always on guard, always on high alert and more nervous than ever. Fearing committal for insanity, my cell phone made me feel safer.

28

Police

BECAUSE I WAS NOW COMING and going without reporting my where-abouts to D, several times, I caught him following me in his pickup. I began to notice a pattern of D speaking to people who I had been speaking to and he would always be sure to tell me in the same sarcastic tone that he had had a real nice visit with them. Years later I would find out from several friends that he was seeking any information I may have shared and couched it in the pitiful-Kate story, the one that portrayed me as such a raving lunatic that nothing I said was reliable. He would open with, "How did Kate seem to you?" Other comments included, "She's going through that woman thing and her mood swings are all over the place," "Whatever you do, don't come to our house 'cause you never know what to expect. Sometimes she runs around the house naked." He would close with the clencher, "I just want the old Kate back." I'm sure he tugged at the heart strings of many who thought the poor guy had a babbling lunatic for a wife that he would care for, and sacrifice for, with death-do-us-part conviction.

To my face, he continued shoving two fingers with his refrain, "Two fuckin' signatures. That's all I need."

With D back in the house after a quick stay at Sam's, which must not have gone well, he resorted to other means of booting me from his family home.

One late summer day in 2011, when his frustration with me boiled over, he called the cops. After hanging up, he raced through the house to let me know the cops were on the way. Laughing wildly, he said they already knew I was crazy, and they were coming to "haul my ass away." I waited, believing D was bluffing. However, this time, he actually followed through on his promise.

Forty-five minutes later, according to the police report, two squad cars pulled up to our house. They appeared to be in no hurry. According to the report, Sunton Police Chief Dick Preston went to the back porch door and was greeted by D, but the truth of the matter was, I ran from the house to get to Preston before D did. I wanted to tell my side of the story. The county officer, who had arrived with Preston, meandered into the garage to talk to D.

"So what's going on Kate?" said Chief Preston.

"D's temper is out of control," I insisted. Preston stared me down with squinty eyes as if to look past me for the truth.

"Are you on any medications?" he asked.

I couldn't understand why he would ask that and told him, 'no.' He gave me that look as if he expected me to come clean.

He asked again, repeating the question louder. Again, I said, 'no.' He tried a different approach.

"Have you seen a doctor lately?" It was then I knew where this line of questioning was headed, and I erupted in sarcasm.

"Let me guess D's been telling you that I'm crazy, right?"

He stammered and stalled replying, "Well, yeah we've talked about you." I flashed back to all the times I saw Preston's squad car pull up to our yard when D would be mowing. D would cut the engine and they would have long conversations with Preston eating up paid hours. I always thought it was ironic that D would be so friendly with him, because D hated cops.

I shook my head with disbelief. In an attempt to keep me calm, Preston switched the topic. He stated the real reason D called the police was to report an apparent burglary.

I guffawed with a fake laugh. "A burglary. Geeze," I said shaking my head.

Preston didn't respond to my resentment, looking down to avoid eye contact.

The angrier I became, the braver I was. "So in this so-called burglary, what the hell was stolen?"

Reading from his clipboard, Preston answered, "D said medallions belonging to his toy collection are missing."

I wondered how long D had been planning this convoluted escapade to put the blame on me and further bolster his argument that I was crazy. Knowing D's tricks and how masterful a magician he was, I shouldn't have been surprised. Now, it was my word against D's and Preston surely didn't believe me, having fed off of years' worth of D's rumor mill.

Preston didn't accuse me of taking them, only assured me if I had, no charges would be filed against me because I was D's wife. I told him I hadn't touched them or taken them. I explained that D and I were going through a divorce, while trying to cohabitate in the same house until our situation was resolved. I also told him that D was making it hell for me, hoping I'd give up and leave, but I wasn't going anywhere, because half of everything D and I owned was mine, in theory.

"Are you sure you didn't take those medallions?" Preston asked again.

"No. I didn't," I answered. "His expensive tractors are worth more with them attached. You're forgetting that D and I are going through a divorce. Iowa law states that half of everything belongs to me," I harped. "It wouldn't make much sense for me to sabotage my half and get less money in the settlement, now would it? It would be like destroying my own property."

"Well, yeah. That makes sense," he said.

I told Preston that D was a mean son-of-a-bitch behind closed doors, but to the public he pretended to be 'Mr. Nice Guy,' acting like some martyr to put up with me. Preston asked if there was abuse going on in my house and I affirmed, citing twenty-five years' worth. He asked if I wanted to press charges against D. Wanting to, but still fearing repercussions, I said 'no,' and told him I thought I could manage until the divorce was settled.

"While Officer Neumeier and D are in the garage, I want to take a look around in your house," said Preston.

As we entered the living room, Preston's eyes caught sight of D's gun cabinet.

"If you think D's so dangerous Kate, maybe we should get the guns out of the house," he said with a laugh.

His mockery of the seriousness forced angry words. "Oh no that's not how he's going to kill me. That'd be too damned obvious."

I stomped to the cellar door and flung it open. My foot spontaneously kicked an empty box I had stored on the top step and it tumbled to the bottom.

"THAT, is how I'm going to die. D's going to shove me down the steps and he said that if that doesn't kill me, he'd bash my head in just to make sure."

I slammed the cellar door shut and glared at him like it would glue my words in place. Preston remained silent for a few seconds. Next, he wanted to know what was in the room with the closed door.

"Oh, that's our bedroom. Excuse me—D's bedroom. I've been sleeping upstairs for months."

As I turned the doorknob, swinging the door open, the blood drained from my face at the sight before us. There, in living color, was a shrine that D had erected to commemorate our wonderful marriage. He had painstakingly collected, framed and hung a myriad of photos of us, including wedding pictures. He had to have searched hard to find existing photos where we appeared to be happy. It was all a show for whoever might trip across our threshold and question his status as a good husband.

Preston looked as surprised as I was.

"Oh, Kate. This doesn't look good," he said. We stood in stunned silence as our eyes searched the feast of glorifying pictures. "Did D know Adam Rowley?" said Preston.

"That's odd that you asked," I said. "D had bragged they had become best of buddies before Adam took his own life." According to local gossip, Adam had been exhibiting odd behavior, isolating himself in his bedroom and being mean to his wife before asphyxiating himself.

"Reminds me a little of Adam—similar patterns of bizarre behavior," said Preston.

At that moment, it felt like I had Preston in my court.

"I want to look at the rest of the house," he said.

Next, I took Preston through the living and dining rooms to what had been the parlor room of the grand old house. At one time, I had filled that room with dolls and Victorian items but as D's toy collection grew, we installed wall to wall shelves in the room to display his boxed toys, getting rid of my doll collection to make more room.

As we entered the room, Preston inquired about some boxes sitting on the carpet and asked if I had put them there.

"No," I said.

"Well, D said you were throwing things in the house. Why are these on the floor?"

"If I was throwing D's toys, there would definitely be holes in the wall or boxes damaged," I said. "Do you see any evidence of that?"

Once the tour of the downstairs was complete, Preston wanted to see the upstairs. I showed him my room with duct tape around the door and told him it was my way of knowing if D had entered my room. In all, I showed Preston the five rooms and two hallways, filled to capacity with toys and in the police report, Preston would note, "I saw only a few items that looked like they belonged to a female in the house."

After scribbling a few more notes on his form, Preston then decided it was time to talk to D.

As I expected, D sat moping on a stool, droopy shoulders and all, role playing, pretending to be the victim. Officer Neumeier sat with him enjoying a soda. I could only imagine D's version of our story, as he glanced at me with puppy-dog eyes of submission. I wanted to puke.

With my radar on high alert, and realizing the magnitude of our situation whereby the police were now involved, and that I had finally spilled the beans about abuse, I was desperate to include every bit of evidence that I would need to try to rally the cops to my side. Figuring it was relative what a drunk D was, I walked over to the refrigerator that D kept in the garage for his beer and I flung it wide to display the beer collection.

"Did D tell you that when he starts drinking, his temper blows?" I said. My voice was so shaky I talked louder to cover it.

"There's nothing wrong with having a few beers," replied Officer Neumeier as he looked at D, and both scoffed at me.

"There is if it makes you lose your temper and you kick the shit out of your wife," I answered, slamming the refrigerator door. Neither Preston nor the county officer responded. I suddenly realized that it didn't look good on my part to carry on as such, because all three men would view me as a wild woman and D as the helpless victim.

Preston, Neumeier, and D walked out of the garage with a casualness that was out of context with the situation.

"Well D, if the medallions were to magically reappear, give us a call," said Preston.

"Yeah. I'll do that. Thanks for coming, you guys," said D, as if they were old friends that D had not seen in years.

Minutes later, the squad cars drove off, leaving D and I alone in a "volatile situation," according to the police record. It also noted, "hopefully, nobody got hurt." In fact, the copy I acquired of that day was quite vague, leaving out everything Preston and I saw and discussed, as if it had never taken place.

That night I began to obsess about the gun cabinet. I knew D's anger could become unleashed with its greatest fury now that I had outright exposed him. The next day after he left the house, I called Preston. I begged him to remove the guns from the house as soon as possible. I told Preston I was feeling less safe by the minute and didn't know when D would return.

Clearly, I wasn't top priority to the local police as Preston's answer came as nothing more than a nonchalant answer, "Well, Kate, I can't get to it this morning. I've got a few personal matters to attend to first. Then, I'll try to get there sometime in the afternoon."

I slammed the cordless phone to the receiver. I called Jenna next. She said she somehow wasn't surprised by the police chief's dismissiveness and told me that she was leaving to drive to Sunton and be a witness, if or when, the Chief showed up to remove the guns. Jenna thought that the problem all along was that I never had witnesses to anything.

Jenna and I waited until late in the afternoon. Preston was a no show. We shook our heads in disgust for the potential seriousness of the situation and the lack of response. Jenna suggested I call Preston back and ask when he was coming. When I did, Preston said he had gotten a call from D and needed to meet with him first as D, too, wanted the guns removed from the house for his safety. It was clever on D's part to have police document his version first. He was covering himself on all angles from what I could see.

An hour later Preston rolled into the driveway. As he walked into the kitchen, I introduced him to Jenna who was sitting at the table. He seemed surprised by her presence but continued.

Preston laid his metal clipboard on the corner of the table and said, "Kate, I do believe there is abuse here."

Finally, validation.

"But there's a problem," he said.

My spirits plummeted.

"D is an employee of the city. He's resided here for a very long time and most of his family also lives in Sunton."

With that, I knew I was sunk.

He explained to Jenna and I that he was going to remove all rifles and ammunition from the gun case. He also removed two more rifles from our attic, per D's direction. After he had itemized everything, he had come back into the kitchen. He slapped a copy of the itemization of all the confiscated guns on the table.

"I'm going to tell you the same thing I told D. If you fear your life is in danger—report to the courthouse tomorrow morning and file a protection order against D."

Minutes later Preston left. Jenna and I chatted for a few more minutes and then she left also, telling me to keep my cell phone charged and hidden at all times. Less than a minute after Jenna's car drove away, D sprang into the house madder than a bull. I found safety, spacing myself from his huffing and pawing. Looking down at the kitchen table, he noticed the yellow copy of the police report of the confiscation of his guns. His entire body inflated with rage. No one messed with his possessions, especially his guns.

"What the fuck is this shit?" shouted D as he scooped the copy from the kitchen table wrinkling it in his shaking fist.

"Preston said you called him to get the guns out of the house. So he did what you told him to do. He removed the guns. That yellow piece of paper is a copy of your complaint," I said, sensing danger and peripherally looking for shelter. I felt the blood drain from my face as I began toward the stairs to clear the room. His face, ears, and neck were ruby red with anger as he beat me to the steps and turned to stand spread-eagle with arms crossed in defiance. I pulled my shoulders tight and tossed my head proudly as I ever so cautiously slithered my way behind him and up the steps. He did not touch me. It made me realize he was scared. I fled to my bedroom, half relieved, half basket case.

That night I slept very little. Months earlier, I had contrived a manner of defense by retrieving a bottle of wasp spray from the garage that I kept near my bed in case D were to lunge at me. I continuously left the hall light on each night, so my next-door neighbor could keep an eye on things per her suggestion. If she didn't see the yellow glow, I instructed her to immediately phone the police for my safety was at risk. I was taking every precaution necessary to keep myself as safe as possible including programing 911 on speed dial for me. I was so technology illiterate at the time, I had to have someone show me how to do it.

After considering Preston's advice about the protection order, Jenna and I decided I should go for it the next morning. She too believed the creeped-out shrine D had erected made him look so twisted that it would be unwise to assume he would do nothing. It was time to be brave and do the inevitable.

I set my alarm for 4:30 a.m. the next day. Full of anxiety, I knew I had to do what I had to do to stay safe. I was so scared D would wake up and intervene to stop me that I didn't even brush my teeth or comb my hair. I grabbed my cell phone and snacks and snuck to the garage. My hands shook badly trying to place the key in the ignition, knowing any minute D could come roaring out the porch door. It was a huge relief I had escaped unharmed. As I headed toward the courthouse in Olson, I kept my eyes on the rearview mirror, convinced D would materialize any minute for I was sure he'd be following.

On my way, I called Jenna in a panic. If anyone could calm my nervousness, it was Jenna. The sound of her voice alone calmed me. She told me when I got to the courthouse to make a list of all the ways D had terrorized me.

It was before 5:30 a.m. when I pulled into the lit parking lot.

29

Protection Order

HAD D NOT SUMMONED THE police, and had Chief Preston not suggested it, it never would have occurred to me to get a protection order. That morning I waited on the steps of the courthouse praying for the order from a judge, and after D showed up to do the same, I was so relieved I had beat him to it.

"For assault and battery," D had declared, making me the aggressor and him the victim. I was not at all surprised and I suspected that Preston had planted the same seed in D.

After some time, the clerk entered the room where I was waiting for word about a judge's signature and said a judge had been located but it might be hours before she arrived. She explained that D was no longer in the courthouse because he had been sent home to await the judge's decision. I was relieved. She asked where I would like to wait as it could take a while for the judge to arrive.

I noticed a small bathroom attached to the judge's chambers and asked if I could stay holed up there until the judge arrived. The guaranteed privacy of the bathroom with a lock on the door, not to mention it was called the Judge's chamber made me feel safe even though D had left the building. But claustrophobia had me taking deep rhythmic breaths. A long window allowing sun rays to light the room helped. I glanced out of it and looked down. There was D on the pavement below standing with Barney near Barney's car. I could see them, but they couldn't see me. Along with them stood D's friend and reserve county officer Shay Turner, who I was sure D summoned for reinforcement. The sight of them sent me into a new cycle of panic. It was three against me. My chances weren't looking good.

To calm my anxiety, I called Jenna again to report the latest. She said she'd send up her prayers and wait for me to call her back.

When I hung up, I noticed D and his friends were gone from the parking lot. Another hour passed. Hyped up on adrenaline, I occupied my time playing scenarios in my head, in the event I wasn't lucky enough to be granted a stay at our house and I would need a backup plan. It was certain to get even uglier, for my words would mean nothing against D's constructed memories and his well-oiled scheme to prove me insane. Not to mention all the witnesses he could roll out to verify my craziness. Hours dragged on, but I never gave up hope as I bargained with God for this one favor.

Someone knocked on the bathroom door. I froze in fear. Not a muscle moved. Then, another rap with someone beckoning me to come out from my hiding place. Still, I didn't answer.

"Kate, it's okay. Unlock the door. The judge has made her decision," said the clerk.

Choking on fear, I was too afraid to ask the decision when the clerk said to follow her. We went into an empty room. I felt ill waiting to hear the decision.

"You got the house," the clerk said. "The judge signed your order and dismissed D's claim against you. You get to stay."

I would have the entire house without D for two weeks. When she handed the document to me, I felt as if I had won the Iowa lottery. I cried tears of joy and told the clerk I wanted to frame the signed protection order. A flood of relief enveloped me. A judge had believed my story. Justice had finally swung my way, at least for now. But would it work? Would D obey it and should I trust it? It was just a piece of paper.

The clerk explained that when the two weeks were up, I could have it renewed but I would have to file the paperwork again. I didn't give a second thought to renewing it for I knew D wouldn't sit idly by, nor would his family, allowing me full reign of myself, if there was anything he or they could do to stop it. I didn't think D would show up at the house in violation of the order, rather, he'd have his family do his dirty work, putting them up to phone calls, hang ups, and drive-bys, and anything else they could think of to push me to my limits. I documented everything which proved helpful when applying for my second protection order.

Knowing D would put up a fight because he would be forced from his house by court order, the chief suspected trouble when the time came to accompany D from the house and off the property. Preston ordered me to remain in the clerk's office until further notice as he was uncertain of D's whereabouts but believed he had gone straight home. As I stood staring out at the side street from the window with the glorious sun warming my face, the clerk's phone rang. I didn't pay attention at first, but her voice became softer. I assumed it was a personal call.

"No sir. Your protection order has been dismissed," replied the clerk.

I knew it was D on the other end of the phone.

It took all day for D to clear the premises before Preston gave the go ahead for me to return. Jenna and her husband hurried to Sunton, to change all the locks for me.

In the meantime, D had already contacted his brother Sam. I noticed someone parked right in front of my driveway later in the day that I had received the signed order. I went out to discover it was D's brother Sam and his wife. They were chatting with my neighbor and appeared to be there only to remind me that D existed in other forms.

30

More Protection Orders

THOUGH I BELIEVED D WAS capable of anything, the protection order made me feel safe for the other eyes on D. It took a while to get used to the calm air in the house that was normally thick with tension. I no longer had to fear entering a room where D was, or flushing a toilet, or reading a book. At times, I basked in the light of hope and as if the fountain of youth sprang from beneath the very ground on which I stood, I felt like my 20-year-old self again.

I had begun the process of exposing the nightmare of my marriage, but the marriage ties had to be severed and it wasn't going to be easy. There was no way to prepare for the onslaught D had promised throughout our marriage in the event I was to leave him. Although he was the one that actually filed the divorce papers, I knew it was going to be hard for him to relinquish a 36-year-old habit of owning a woman. It was sure to turn into an ugly brawl.

I tried to prepare myself, learning to be much more mindful of my surroundings. Always on high alert, I watched over my shoulder, became obsessed with locking things, conversed with my neighbors to see if they had seen anything suspicious, checked my tires for flats, and continued surveilling traffic on my street.

Though divorce was unchartered territory, I now had a support system including my brother Lee and my friends Jenna and Jay. The three strategized future plans looking for housing that would suit my needs. Their moral support was the answer to my prayers and they were the only three directly in my court.

Meanwhile, I secured a lawyer to represent me. Lauren Hoffman began negotiating with D's attorney, Mark Foley, over temporary monthly support. Because I valued Lee's and Jenna's opinions on financial matters, both accompanied me to Lauren's office often. It was on one of those appointments that D's silver truck followed us. I documented the intimidation. Months later, D would use the excuse to a judge that it was just a coincidence that he needed groceries, traveling the 50 miles to Duly's large Walmart Center.

As the days passed quickly and the two weeks were up, another judge granted the renewed order. He based it on my complaints of D's family driving by and because D told a mutual acquaintance that he wanted to bury me six feet under. This time the judge renewed the second protection order, giving me an entire month's bliss.

When the second Order of Protection expired, Lauren and I had prepared to argue for the third protection order. We were equipped with a letter from my therapist and counselor at Clearview Center as well as documentation of D's family and friends driving past the house.

The hearing for the third protection order was the biggest show down of all. Most of D's immediate family showed up including his mother, who hobbled into the courtroom with her walker, from the nursing home where she resided. A part of me felt sorry for her because her maternal commitment couldn't allow her to see the real man. She knew D better than anyone as I had witnessed D mentally and verbally abusing her as well over the years. Deep down, I felt she knew the truth.

D wanted his house back so badly that he agreed to pay me a temporary amount of spousal support until the divorce was settled. He also was desperate for me to drop the protection order because it prevented him from driving city trucks at his part-time job with the city of Sunton.

Their offer of support was an amount that was above what I thought they would offer. However, they made this contingent upon both my moving out by December 1, 2011, and upon my dropping the protection order. I refused. I needed my protection order. I did, however, agree not to press charges. In the pre-hearing meeting, my lawyer went back and forth with negotiations and at one point Lauren returned angry after they played a dirty card.

"Why didn't you tell me about all the police reports they have on you?" she steamed, with her hand on her hip. I was flabbergasted. I had no idea what she meant.

"They're saying they have police reports about you wandering on the highway in a confused state," she said. "And they have a county officer prepared to take the stand about it, Kate," she said like she was scolding me.

"I have no blessed idea what you're talking about," I said, stumped but not surprised by the antics and definitely panicked by the new fresh hell.

Lauren squinted at me as if trying to see the truth. "If they can produce these reports, this is not going to make you look good."

I struggled for the answer but was clueless. I didn't know if they were serious, or if it was a cheap scare tactic in the middle of the support negotiation. I should have asked to see the reports. I should have asked if she had seen the reports. I should have been in the room with her. Instead, I froze. I deferred to her as the expert and assumed she was protecting my best interest.

Despite the veiled threat, we continued to negotiate. In the end, they agreed to give me $1,000 a month until the divorce was finalized, even though I refused to drop the protection order. D clearly wanted his house back. To this day, I kick myself for not pressing charges against D for crimes he committed against my humanity.

Because I held onto the protection order card with a vengeance and because it was about to expire, the judge presiding that day granted me the third protection order. This time for a whole year. I was exhausted when I left the courtroom, but I squared my shoulders and held my head high, for my voice had mattered.

Per our agreement of that day, I was to move out of our house by the first of December. My plan was to move to my brother Lee's farm until I could get my affairs settled and make decisions.

Meanwhile, D's frivolous complaints upped my attorney's bill. Of all the ridiculous things D found to complain about, accusing me of taking his underwear topped the list. At first, I thought Lauren was kidding when she angrily phoned, questioning me.

"Are you fucking kidding me?" I said and couldn't quite stifle the chuckle that happened mid-sentence.

"Kate, this isn't funny. Did you take his underwear when you moved from the premises?"

"Hell no. But, I sure wish I had, so I could burn them along with my marriage certificate when the divorce is finalized."

"Seriously, Kate, do you have his underwear?" Lauren questioned.

"Seriously, Lauren. I don't have his underwear. I took very few possessions with the exception of my personal items. I gave you photos of everything I removed from the house," I said.

"Ok. Look, face it, divorces are ugly and petty," said Lauren, resigning herself to the fact that she wasn't going to get anywhere else with me. "Don't worry about the underwear. That's often a tactic to distract from a bigger issue."

It so irritated me that D was driving up my attorney's fees on purpose that I decided to play his game. I had discovered that D still had not removed my name from our joint checking account and that there was still a few hundred dollars left in the account. I came up with the brainstorm to contract two scrawny teenage boys to do the job of mowing the lawn that seemed of such great concern to D. I supplied them with D's primed and polished lawnmowers and they went to work chopping the grass with sweat equity. Hours later, after water breaks, potty breaks, smoke breaks, and just plain breaks, the lawnmowers finally ran out of gas. The yard looked more like a hayfield by the time they were done, and they were physically exhausted, but I was quite pleased with the results. I had rarely ever written checks because D did all the check writing, and I was scared to death, but it was the most fun I had ever had.

Instead of storing D's expensive lawn mowers in the garage, I allowed them to sit outside in the driveway to weather for a few days, for I knew it would get back to D by way of the nosy neighbor across the street. Sure enough, I got a call from Chief Preston saying that D kept calling to complain that the lawn mowers were sitting out. I let them sit for another few days before I brought them in.

Between writing a check to the lawn boys for $150 and a check to Walmart for $300 for a shopping spree of household items I would need in my new home, I imagined D's eyes bugging out when he saw the bank statement. Each purchase was accompanied by my third finger salute to D.

31

Ava's Betrayal

THE HUMIDITY THAT SUMMER SEEMED to fuel the divorce flame and contribute to flaring tempers. Though money was no longer an immediate concern due to the provided spousal support, the divorce dragged on due to the petty games on both our parts.

It would have taken a trial to uncover all the inconsistencies and lies in D's answers on the interrogatories, such as his insistence that the $64,130.50 toy collection was worth only a few thousand dollars and that they were all gifted to him.

D had also claimed that he came into the marriage with $25,000. I don't recall him coming into our marriage with anything more than a couple of thousand, certainly not a big chunk. One day, I received a phone call from my attorney asking me why I hadn't disclosed that to her. I was incredulous and told her that it was completely untrue. You would think as my attorney, Lauren would know that bank records don't go back that far but she suggested I go to the bank to see if they had records to prove D's claim. I couldn't understand why the onus wasn't upon him to prove that it was true. Sure enough, the bank informed me that they don't keep records past seven years.

Lauren appeared to be trying to speed up the process and didn't want to call them out on anything. All I had wanted was to split things up equitably and go our separate ways. I wasn't asking for more than my half. I was even prepared to give D more than his share just to end it all but he continued dragging the divorce on trying to muscle every penny he could out of my future. And, the bad news kept coming.

One Sunday morning my sister Ava called under the guise that she wanted to offer her copy machine so that I could run copies of documentation for my settlement hearing. When I arrived at her house, it didn't take long to figure out that she wanted to purge guilt. She launched into a story about how, six months earlier, her trucker husband, Dan, believed his load was over the weight limit. Pulling into a weigh station several miles from Sunton with his semi, Dan found D's brother, Sam, working that day at the co-op. Making small talk, Sam joked to Dan that cops found me walking the highway again. I was allegedly confused as to where I was, so law enforcement called D. Sam allegedly smirked to Dan as if he found the whole thing quite comical.

I was stunned into silence. It felt like the proverbial pet rabbit boiling in the pot—the moment when you realize that nothing is safe, and something has been undermining you all along. Now, D's threat at the hearing for the third protection order, claiming he had police reports on me, made sense. As I was walking to get exercise, D was painting me as delusional and unable to find my way back home. For months, I had had an eerie feeling that people were staring at me or pretending they didn't know me when they did. Now I knew it was because I was supposedly batshit crazy. It was more evidence that D had been laying the ground work for getting me committed to a mental ward, in case I got bucky and spilled the beans on his abuse of me.

I didn't understand why Ava would wait half a year to share information that would aid me in my case against D. I wondered if she thought I was crazy too. To top it off, Ava then called back a few hours later to tell me that Dan had recanted his story and claimed that the entire conversation between Sam and Dan never happened. Aside from the staggering realization that D's deviousness was even more twisted than I realized, now I wondered if my own sister was going to turn her back on me too. Though she had helped me, she wanted to ignore what was going on.

I stewed for days, trusting no one but Jenna, Jay, and Lee. Then, even Lee seemed to want to turn away, too squeamish to look at the bloody mess of my life, as I dug for information about what D had been telling them all those years. My family made it clear that they wanted nothing to do with my divorce and repeatedly told me to stop talking about it and move on.

I also knew I couldn't rely on the chief of police. Covering his own butt, his typed police report was a vague version of his visit to our house that day. Missing were my concerns that D would shove me down the cellar steps and bash my head. There was nothing in the report about guns in the house. However, he made sure to include the question as to whether or not I was on any medication as well as my answer in the negative.

Just when I thought my family was sick of my drama, my brother Lee came forward and did a remarkable thing. Because I had no collateral and no credit history, the bank would not give me a loan to buy a house. Lee purchased a home for me and we agreed that I would live in the small two-bedroom house for as long as I was able to take care of it on my own.

32

Counseling

IN THE FINAL MONTHS THAT I resided at D's house, I dreaded answering my cell phone knowing it was Lauren with a new steaming pile. We continued to argue badly. I felt she lacked wisdom because she was young and inexperienced. To cover herself, she repeatedly used the excuse, "a judge won't go for that," dismissing anything productive that could have helped my case. She had used that excuse so many times, I wondered if she was scared of going to court. I begged her to stand up for me.

"They're backing us into a corner because you're letting them," I said repeatedly.

She touted her experience representing victims of domestic abuse, which made it a huge oversight on her part in failing to advise me to seek therapy for such. It had never dawned on me that I needed therapy, except the time D insisted I needed it to create an uptick in our sexual life. My head had been stuck in the sand for so long that I didn't even recognize myself as a victim.

It was only when my sister Ava suggested that I should be on some medication for depression that I came to realize that I might benefit from counseling. I ended up seeking help at a local abuse center that offered free counseling for domestic abuse and sexual assault victims.

I had several sessions with the first therapist, Melanie, who transferred me to another therapist named Mollie in Duly who dealt strictly with sexual assault cases. I learned from them that abusers refuse to give up control over their victims and that the most dangerous time was during my separation. Working with local authorities, Melanie kept close tabs on my safety. She had dealt with many cases of men portraying their wives as crazy and said it was common.

I had no support system and it made me perfect prey. According to Mollie, this was typical. With no support, the victim spirals into depression, believing they will never get out of their dangerous dilemma. Many give up, turning to alcohol, drugs, gambling, even promiscuity to numb mental anguish as their abuse continued. I swore I'd never touch such vices, but there were days I wanted to light a cigarette to ease my anxiety. I felt good denying my craving because I felt in control of something.

The longer I attended therapy, the more confident I became that I was not to blame for the abuse D perpetrated. I had made every attempt to be a good wife and partner to D. I even gave up motherhood for D. I was always apologizing for things, just to keep peace, unsure why I was sorry. Adjusting, adapting, and enduring had become my way of life as I'd known it, which was D's way only.

Although D filed for divorce, he did everything in his power to thwart the process. He enjoyed controlling me, my attorney, and his attorney and making my life as miserable as possible. It wasn't me he wanted, it was the control that made him feel powerful with every little victory he won over me and Lauren.

D's antics included violating the Writ of Injunction from early in the divorce. He closed our checking account and removed my name from several life insurance policies. When I discovered I was no longer the beneficiary, we hard pressed him to take out another new life insurance policy for $100,000 with me as sole beneficiary. Lauren and I demanded that it state in the decree that if for any reason, D would remove my name from the policy, I could take him back to court at his expense. D and his attorney begrudgingly agreed to this or Lauren and I would have pressed charges against D for violating court order. He could be looking at jail time and D knew it.

I moved into my new home in Manley December 2011, after staying several weeks with my brother Lee and his wife. I had limited funds but had learned to make do by decorating my home with garage sale finds and Goodwill bargains.

Frugality was something I had perfected through the years with D and now those skills came in handy as I built my new life.

My house was a perfect match for my existing health problems. There were no steps so that if I ever required a wheelchair again or had to use a walker, it would be easier.

Jenna invited me often to accompany her during her errand runs, to get me more acquainted with Manley and all it had to offer. I introduced myself to the neighbors and made sure they were aware of the Order of Protection I had on D. Members of my family stopped in to visit from time to time, as if to check my welfare, but they were consistent in their refrain, as if it had been discussed in a group setting, that I should move on and stop belaboring my situation. This, while my divorce raged, and I couldn't move forward without a judgment. I built an emotional wall to protect myself from them.

However, Lee and I became closer as I opened up, wanting him to understand the silence of spousal abuse. We talked for hours as I poured out my secrets. Each day became a new day of growth as the more I purged my story, the easier it became to uncover the truth.

With my computer up and running in my new home, and without fear of some-one looking over my shoulder, I began journaling about my life and marriage. It didn't take long before I became frustrated by my lack of education and inability to express myself to the degree I wanted. I began reading every book I could find. I also studied writing books and became intrigued with the idea of writing a memoir about my abusive marriage. Several friends had told me it would be a good book and a necessary one as far as helping others. Once that thought was established, I was obsessed with the notion and it became my livelihood.

33

Free

TEN MONTHS FROM THE DATE D filed for divorce in March of 2012, my attorney and I met with D and his attorney at the county courthouse in Manley for the settlement hearing. I insisted we sit in separate rooms. As tension mounted, I began to think Lauren was falling for D's mind games. Twice, she entered the room where I was holed up to give me items D wanted me to have. These were items that he had taken and hidden before the first protection order. It was strategic on D's part as if giving them back at the settlement hearing would win him a personality contest. Still, Lauren fell for it and commented on how nice it was of him. Needless to say, it infuriated me and because she was under the false assumption that it was nice of him, she acted as if I was being an unreasonable wretch.

Every time she entered our room, it was a new argument as she kept pushing me to cave to their demands. She seemed to have run out of time and continued to use the excuse, "the judge won't go for that." Whether she was right or not, every time she said it, my desire grew to hear the words directly from the judge himself. We moved closer to trial. In order to force my hand to settle, Lauren warned me of the great expense involved in a trial, floating a $2,000 per hour price tag. I wasn't sure what she meant by this and didn't ask, but it scared me.

For hours, the four of us haggled back and forth about everything. All along, Lauren had led me to believe I was entitled to further spousal support. D refused to give me any. Lauren refused to fight for it and in the end, I had to agree to it or go through a costly trial. Divorce was an expensive education and one that taught me that there was no such thing as fair.

After the settlement hearing was over, I returned home while Lauren finished paperwork with Foley and D. According to what Lauren told me later, D tried to hit on her in front of Foley.

"You know Lauren, if we had met under different circumstances," Lauren said, imitating D. "I would have bought you a drink." He then went on to ask her to drop the protection order against him. It was the first time that Lauren felt the full impact of D's natural tendency to manipulate.

We divided up our list of stocks and CDs and D got to choose what he wanted first. According to Lauren, this was because he was the petitioner. D then insisted it would take him three months to cash in all of our investments for the sake of dividing them. He waited until the last day of the deadline. D also got the title to the house, all the furnishings, his pickup truck, two muscle cars, the entire toy collection and a garage filled with $29,000 worth of tools.

More than I wanted 'things,' I wanted my independence. The closer I came to getting it, the more anxious I became to get it at any cost. It wasn't about the material items as much as never being his property again. I surely didn't need old reminders of him haunting me further as freedom was so close to my reach. I got the title to the 2010 Chevy Impala, a sofa, computer, desk, chair, and one small TV.

Finally, the day came to cut the marriage bond officially and sign the divorce decree. In June of 2012, I would finally own all of me and be rid of the monkey on my back. I feared going to the courthouse. I was sure D's family would be there to perform theatrical, show-stopping intimidation.

Lauren stated there was no need for me to be at the courthouse to sign the divorce decree. She said she'd drive to my house if I could get a witness for signatures. After all necessary paperwork was signed, Lauren left again for the Manly courthouse to obtain the opposing's signatures for finalizing the process. However, she was caught off guard.

According to Lauren, she was met at the top of the courthouse steps with scowls and stares by D's friend Barney and several of D's sisters. His whole tribe had arrived for the finale. Lauren was relieved that I hadn't appeared.

I could only image how disappointed they all were that I didn't appear. Great theatrics ensued. At one point D stormed out of the courthouse refusing to sign documents over some small issue. He and his attorney also threatened to file charges against me because I had copied a life insurance document from D's policy while I still had access to it. At one point, one of D's sisters blurted, "This divorce is not happening. We're not signing anything and we'll start from the beginning again."

It makes sense to me now as to why his sister would say that, as D had cried on his families' shoulders for months before the divorce was in full swing, complaining that I had taken him to the cleaners. At one point D had accused me of planning on winning his mother's house in the divorce. I can only assume that he directed his family to believe the same, because they acted as if I was wrenching their mother's home from their hands. This was an absurd notion, proven by the fact that three years after the divorce was finalized, D inadvertently discovered that my name was still on the deed to his mother's house. It was an oversite on everyone's part in the division of property in the divorce and I could have claimed it was half mine, but I didn't. I signed the paperwork to have it deeded back to D with absolutely no desire to stake claim.

After much haggling over many issues, we finally reached the point where we signed the blessed decree. This didn't mean I was free of D and his games. For the next three months I was financially handcuffed while D took his sweet time transferring funds to me.

Instead of reveling in my newfound freedom, I was depressed and panicky as the reality of my life set in. I now had to start over and go it alone. As I sat in D's imposed limbo, I poured over the years lost, pummeling myself for being so naïve.

During that time, I had to force myself to take steps in transitioning to a new life. I took walks, ate healthier, and took vitamin supplements, hoping to improve my overall appearance as I tried to fend off the debilitating effects of Fibromyalgia. As the months passed, my hair began to grow in the patches of baldness in the back of my head. I began to gain confidence that I had control over my health. I became more mindful of my surroundings. Colors seemed brighter. I became more interested in what other women were wearing, how they styled their hair and how they did their makeup. I listened to conversations everywhere I went.

Over time, I became grateful for what I had, rather than sorrowful for what I didn't have.

The day came when Foley's office sent a personal check from D in the amount of $27,305 for final settlement to Laurens's office. It was that day my official new life began. I was 57 years old when I was reborn.

34

Aftermath

THOUGH IT WAS ALL OVER, D's charades continued as if he couldn't let go of me. His sisters were still cruising my house to taunt me. D and his friend Barney would also drive by in violation of the protection order but I couldn't prove it unless I had a video camera. In one instance, while walking down the sidewalk in Manley, I found myself walking head on into one of D's sisters. As I passed her, she shoved me from the side while snorting like a pig. Another time, my sister Ava was also shoved by the same bullying sister in a grocery store. None of these incidents alone were enough to warrant calling the police, and I had been warned by a local police dispatcher not to report every little incident, as too many calls have the effect of decreasing interest on the part of the police.

With the courts, law enforcement, neighbors and friends fully aware of my situation, I continued spreading word of my protective order knowing there was safety in numbers. Arming myself with documentation including a permit to carry, I was prepared to renew the next restraining order.

The day came in September of 2012, when I entered the Clark County Courthouse with Lauren, determined to renew the protection order for the fourth time. D's family, including Barney and Chief Preston, all stood together as if in solidarity.

Support from my brother Lee, my godchild Terry, Melanie and an armed security guard eased my jitters as we gathered in a small room, distancing ourselves from the loud D-mob that was loitering in the hallway and causing commotion. They were conversing openly as if they were at a picnic.

I found it ironic that D, who threatened and terrorized my life, found it necessary to employ his siblings and friends in the matter of intimidating me.

After reviewing my documentation along with a support letter from my therapist and counselor, the judge renewed the protection order for the fourth time, for another full year. I was informed by a clerk of court, much later, that it was unusual to accumulate that many restraining orders against one person.

Over the next few weeks, I decided to satisfy my curiosity as to the contents of all police records and logs involved in my case. I needed to know for personal closure just how far back D had spun claims of my insanity.

In October of that same year, Lauren and I subpoenaed local and county records pertaining to D and/or me. According to their response, an in-house search of county records under both our names was conducted and that no records were found. I was suspicious as to why there were no records. I was unable to find out just how long I had been crazy.

35

Closure

D BRAINWASHED ME, MANIPULATED ME, lied to me, beat me, isolated me, restrained me financially, deprived my life of love, children, and grandchildren and drove a wedge between me and my family. But the offense that burns the most, that shocked me beyond all because of the extent of the deceit, was that he damaged my name and reputation with the stigma of mental illness.

That stigma is inescapable. No one looks at you the same. Because people don't trust you, they shun you. They walk on eggshells around you believing you may fly off the handle. Your good word means nothing. I felt like a fool for never seeing it until it had advanced to a sophisticated level. For whatever reason, no one came forward to tell me what D was feeding them. Above all, I hated D for this.

After spending my early life attempting to build a good name for myself, my reputation had always been important to me. I cared what people thought of me. Like anyone, I wanted to be liked. Upon realizing the full extent of D's destruction to my reputation, I made it my mission to earn it back.

I know that divorces are mean and ugly and bring out the worst in us. Both parties bicker over pettiness and lose friendships and relationships in the process. But D's insistence on portraying me as insane, and the length of time he worked on this plot went above and beyond the typical divorce nastiness.

On the advice of my therapist, I began journaling. Armed with my interest in writing my story, and though it felt like a foreign concept at first to roll the honesty out on paper, once I started writing, the words poured as if I couldn't vomit the poison fast enough. Mollie had told me that this would aid the healing process. It did.

Seven years have since passed since my marriage ended. I still own the same Chevy Impala. It's the only material reminder I have of my marriage to D. I think back to that August morning in 2011, when I sat locked in the car at the courthouse waiting to file the first protection order. That spins other memories of an era wasted, but the Chevy has a place in my heart. It anchors me by reminding me of where I was, to make me grateful for where I am.

Armed with the wisdom that comes from making bad choices and mistakes, I now go forth with conviction to live the rest of my days of my own accord. The freedom that came to me in the end was something that felt so strange at first that I didn't know how to accept it. I felt scared and anxious about being alone, fearful of a void, until I realized there was no void. Now, nothing and no one will stand in the way of my free choice again.

I have found love. Simon is someone I have known longer than I knew D. D and I had even been friends with Simon and his wife for many years. When both our marriages ended, Simon and I formed a friendship that eventually blossomed into more. He is a patient, kind man who has shown great reserves of love and respect. He has even helped bring my story to fruition and the bond I have with Simon feels normal and healthy. Though it has taken me time to believe that such a love could exist, I feel lucky and grateful that I found love at all in the later years of my life, much less a love that feels so good.

I hope to lead by example, excavating my secrets here to write a memoir. I hope to give someone else what I wished I'd had—strength and courage. I hope to set others free to rebuild a life and a name. Though the past is always present, and can make me sad, every day that I awake in the absence of distress is a great new day. I greet the sun with a smile and a deep cleansing breath that comes from knowing I'm free to be me. I have found reserves of energy I didn't know I had. It is an energy like water that seeks its level and can't be contained, like a life that starts late and must pack in plenty in a short amount of time.

Epilogue

WITHOUT THE LOVING SUPPORT FROM my brother Lee, and Jenna and her husband Jay, rescuing me from a hostile marriage, I'm certain my memoir would have never been written. Never faltering, they stood by me as I delayed the inevitability of divorce. When the first of many Orders of Protection were issued, their alliance eased the difficulty to the start of my new beginning.

I am most grateful to be blessed with newfound freedom. After 7 years, it's still as fresh and new as the day strings were severed from my marriage. I continue to rebuild my life to its fullest potential. Looking forward to each new day brings new meaning and a sense of purpose. I have learned to like myself again and love me for who I have become. Empowerment has exhilarated me to become an advocate against domestic violence.

In retrospect, there were many cautionary signs, red flags, and indications of my emotional abuse that led to physical altercations that no one noticed or refused to see. Being alienated and isolated within the storm of domestic violence, fear won over freedom. Adjusting and adapting, I'd become complacent to the mistreatment, accepting it as normal behavior.

Prevalent everywhere, spousal abuse has touched not only my life, but the lives of loved ones in my community as well. Allowing my voice to be heard through my memoir, it is my hope a deeper understanding capitulates others to support loved ones who are silencing their shameful secrets. It takes but one person to validate claims to begin the process of leaving an abuser . . . and healing.